WE'RE ALL DOING OUR BEST

*FINDING GOD'S HEALING, GRACE AND
TRUTH THROUGH EXAMINATION OF
OUR STORIES*

I0093169

BY TASHA PAGE

Copyright © 2022 TASHA PAGE.

All Rights Reserved.

No part of this publication may be reproduced, distributed, or transmitted in any form or by any means, including photocopying, recording, or other electronic or mechanical methods, or by any information storage and retrieval system without the prior written permission of the publisher, except in the case of very brief quotations embodied in critical reviews and certain other noncommercial uses permitted by copyright law.

CHEAT SHEET

בְּרֵאשִׁית

"IN THE BEGINNING"
INTRODUCTION

"He has told you, O man, what is good;
and what does the Lord require of you
but to do justice, and to love kindness,
And to walk humbly with your God"
Micah 6:8 (ESV)

If you are anything like I am, you have cried out to God at one point in time or another, asking Him "What do you want from me? Why am I here? What is your will for my life? Is there a point to our existence down here?" I mean, surely there is a purpose that the layperson can grasp without going to seminary or becoming a philosopher?

The first time I heard the verse Micah 6:8 I was sitting in my therapist's office. I was celebrating about eight months of sobriety at the time, except every day felt like a struggle instead of a celebration. I had recently gotten out of an emotionally toxic relationship with a man I started dating in rehab who was an H&I speaker (There are so many things wrong with that scenario, but more on that in a later chapter). I worked overnight as a CNA at a local nursing home at close to the minimum wage to provide for my two boys and was physically and mentally exhausted. I was almost at the end of my rope, and the excitement of my newfound born-again relationship with Christ was wearing off when I realized there wasn't a system to how God works so that I could manipulate Him into making my life perfect.

What struck me after she finished reading the verse to me was the 6:8 part of the verse because my birthday is June 8th (I am self admittedly egotistical like that at times). I asked her to reread it, and that's when it felt like a lightning bolt had struck me. All those times when I was crying out to God in the pit of my pain asking Him what He wanted from me, He had already put the answer in front of my face:

> *"He has told you, O man, what is good;*
> *and what does the Lord require of you"*

I could almost hear Him lovingly saying in a Billy Mays voice: "Hey woman! Do you want to know what is good and what my purpose for you is? Do you want to know what I want from you? I have already told you the answer, but keep reading. There's more!" Who doesn't want more? Umm… yes please! So on to the next verse…

> *"but to do justice, and to love kindness,*
> *And to walk humbly with your God"*

It was at that moment that something clicked. My glorious God, who created all of the heavens and the earth, loved me enough to make my birthday June 8th so that Micah 6:8 would stand out like a lightbulb in a dark season when I didn't want to live anymore. He is a personal God concerned with the big and the small things. This revelation had given me a small glimpse of hope in a dark season as to what my next steps should be. In one tiny verse, He had laid out three simple steps to a joyful existence: 1) Try to do the next right thing 2) Love my neighbors, and 3) Develop a personal relationship with Jesus Christ instead of seeking only head knowledge about Christ.

Simple! Done! Now I'm a perfect person with no problems, and I've come to tell you peasants how to accomplish this as well. NOT! This event took place almost three years ago, and I'm still a hot mess at times. But at least I'm a hot mess with hope now, and I know that I am deeply and profoundly loved.

The part of the verse that sticks out most to me is the "walk humbly part." In Dave Adamson's *52 Hebrew Words Every Christian Should Know*,[1] one of the Hebrew words for humble is *anavah* (H6038) which can be translated as "to occupy your God-given space." I've always struggled with that concept. The older I get though, the more I realize that God probably doesn't have a divine destiny carved out in stone for my life. He cares more about the walk. God has been walking with us since the beginning in Genesis 3:8-13, "And they heard the sound of the LORD God walking in the garden in the cool of the day, and the man and his wife hid themselves from the presence of the LORD God

9

among the trees of the garden. But the LORD called to the man and said to him, "Where are you?" And he said, "I heard the sound of you in the garden, and I was afraid, because I was naked, and I hid myself". He said, "Who told you that you were naked? Have you eaten of the tree of which I commanded you not to eat?" The man said, "The woman whom you gave me to be with me, she gave me the fruit of the tree, and I ate." Then the LORD God said to the woman, "What is this that you have done?" The woman said, "The serpent deceived me, and I ate."

You can almost hear the agony in God's voice when he says, "What is this that you have done?" This was the defining event in the garden that would lead so many of His children away from walking humbly with Him. Away from his greatest desire. They were forced into a broken world because sin separates us from Him. He is so holy He can't stand in the presence of it. Internally, we know our hearts are infected, so we have a tendency to attempt to hide from Him due to our shame, pain, and disappointment. We listen to the lies the serpent feeds us, which shapes who we are and how we interact with the world. A lot of who we are results from the environment that we are raised in. It might seem normal to us, but it's not always beneficial. Our spirits cry out because we subconsciously know deep in our DNA that we were built for more. We were built to walk humbly with our Father. We were built to worship.

The Hebrew concept of worship was different than ours is today. It wasn't just singing and dancing at church. It incorporated so much more than those two things. Everything that they did was an act of worship. They dedicated all the work of their hands to him. As well as their interactions with family and friends. They studied and debated His written word in their everyday conversations. The words they spoke and the thoughts they thought were all meant to be dedicated to God. All of their heart and soul and mind. It's hard to keep your thoughts on Jesus. At times that goal seems impossible. Yet He doesn't expect that level of perfection from us. That command didn't come from Him. When we aren't listening to Him, we have to ask ourselves whose voice are we listening to? I have "Who told you that...?" tattooed on my foot, as a reminder that I need to be conscientious where my worship is directed to. The serpent and the world will tell me that I am not smart, pretty, kind (pick your adjective here) enough. We are being fed a constant stream of lies that our best isn't good enough. We internalize all of these lies, and they start to form our identities over time and we forget how we were meant to occupy our God-given space in this world. We lose hope. There is nothing worse than lost hope.

Mankind has been creating inspiring tales since the beginning of time because we need inspiration as much as we do food or oxygen. Word by word, sentence by sentence, chapter by chapter, we find life-giving nourishment to persevere throughout our daily struggles in our shared stories. Words are the way God speaks to us. We each are co-authoring a story with God, except many of us are co-authoring this story without awareness of the other Authors contributions. Or our place in the saga. We are like actors trying to forever run the whole show, forever trying to arrange the stage and the other actors.[2] We get mad and resentful when the play doesn't come across as we envisioned, and we pile up resentments in our hearts. These drag us down and steal our hope slowly killing us.

The way back to life is to get out of autopilot and to admit we need help. We have to surrender our lives to the editor, and then go through the process of examining our life story with Him. It is in this examination that we find God's healing, grace, and truth. We learn to walk humbly with Him again, one day at a time. That's all He ever wanted from us in the first place.

Throughout the pages of this book, I would like to share parts of my story with you in the hopes that you will begin to examine your own. I understand that relationships are like bank accounts, and I have to earn your trust. Hopefully, my openness, honesty, and transparency will earn the right to speak what I have learned to be God's truth to you. I don't say these things from the mountaintop, and I'm far from perfect. I come to you in the trenches as we fight against the harsh realities of this life. I thank you for your time, and I pray that you find something within the content of these pages that inspires you and gives you hope.

א

SPIRITUAL EKG

"If your hate could be turned into electricity,
it would light up the whole world."
-Nikola Tesla

"Ladies and gentlemen, fasten your seatbelts. Please keep
your hands and feet inside the vehicle at all times. Your
safety is my top priority, and this ride may get a little bumpy
at times".

This first chapter might seem a little turbulent,
depending on your world point of view. Full
disclaimer, I view the Bible as the true and living Word
of God, and this book was written through that lens.
BEFORE YOU PUT DOWN THE BOOK, I promise I'm
not trying to go all fire and brimstone preacher on you.
I'm all about grace and truth, and I will love you even
if you disagree with me. However, to set the
precedence for this entire book, some foundational
work needs to be done to clear the way. The topics are
profound but deserve to be discussed. I also happen to
get squirreled easily. Some minds aren't wired to think
on a linear path. But I promise that if I bring a subject
up, it is relevant to the main point, and I will circle
back to connect it. My recommendation if you start to
feel squirmy is that you throw one hand up (you need
the other to hold the book), take a deep breath of the
Ruach HaKodesh (The Holy Spirit), and enjoy the ride.

Life is not perfect

Many adjectives can describe our first breath to our last, but perfect is definitely not one of them. At the time I'm writing this book, there are almost eight billion people on the planet. Metaphorically speaking, it sounds as if the world is groaning at times. People legitimately groan about serious things such as war, poverty, and destruction. They also groan about small minor annoyances like pumpkin spice lattes made with almond milk instead of oat milk (okay, maybe I'm the only one that does that). We're comparable to modern-day versions of the Israelites on our own wilderness journeys, walking around the wilderness complaining and crying out to God about how life isn't good enough. All the while, those of us with social media accounts frequently post picture-perfect representations of our life stories so that we can make others groan about how they don't have as good of a life as we do. It's exhausting. The incessant groaning is an attempt to find some relief from the stress that we feel inside and from all the negativity that surrounds us all daily. Contrary to Winston Churchill's opinion, I think it is helpful to point out here that we are all doing our best given our circumstances.

That last statement may incite annoyance or even anger. You might be asking, "How can you possibly say a murderer on death row or a pedophile is doing their best?!" I'm going to double down and would reiterate that even those we consider to be the most detestable examples in human history are all doing *their* personal best to get through each day in this rough wilderness terrain where we have found ourselves. Before you break out the tar and feathers, at least make it through chapter three, so I can explain myself a little better. Everybody has a story, and no one was born precisely the person they see in the mirror today.

A significant amount of groundbreaking research has been done in the field of social neuroscience in the twenty-first century. Daniel Goleman's *Social Intelligence: The New Science of Human Relationships* is an excellent resource for this subject matter. He states, "Neuroscience has discovered that our brain's very design makes it sociable, inexorably drawn into an intimate brain-to-brain linkup whenever we engage with another person. That neural bridge lets us affect the brain -and so the body-of everyone we interact with, just as they do us."[1]

In other words, even the most seemingly insignificant daily interactions have the power to mold and shape who we are as people. Our environments and relationships affect us over time through "neuroplasticity," which sculpts our neurons and synaptic connections through repeated experiences. Depending on who we interact with, our relationships affect us positively and negatively. Unfortunately, we happen to live in a fallen world that bears little resemblance to the bliss found in our original surroundings at the time of creation. All the groaning discussed above can be contagious and wreak havoc on our spirits. It breaks our hearts, then we break other people's hearts, who break our hearts again. The way we interact with the people in our lives may seem normal to us, but even the best of our relationships have flaws. They are far from the perfection that God had intended for us when He created us to walk with Him in the garden.

First Coffee, Then World Domination...

Each day that we wake up, we are presented with a clean slate of twenty-four hours that we get to decide how we will write the story of our lives. Although I must admit that if I don't get my alone time with Jesus and my coffee first thing in the morning, then my odds of writing my story in a shapeless orange/striped jumpsuit increase exponentially. Just saying. I make it a point to carve out time for those things, even though some mornings I would much rather sleep. I must learn how to surrender to the Spirit and dominate my fleshly urges. The Word says we were created to have dominion over the things on the earth around us. (Genesis 1:26) Created in God's image, that's what we were designed to do. In the time of Adam and Eve, it was the fish in the sea and the birds in the heavens. There were no other people yet, and they did not have knowledge of good and evil. Sin hadn't entered the world at this point. But in today's age, it is present. That, my friends, is wherein the real problem lies.

There are other people in the world now, and all people have inherited a sinful nature from our original ancestors, Adam and Eve. We were created without knowledge of evil to co-dominate our environments while walking humbly with God. However, now we tend to want complete executive control of our lives and the lives of everyone else around us. Most of us have struggled all our life trying to control the uncontrollable, believing that the right combination of actions would guarantee the outcomes we desire.

From the time we are born, our brains start collecting our experiences and forming an operational system to interpret how the world works. Then we use that system of operation as a golden standard for all of those around us and hold them accountable for behaving within the rules within that system. We expect others to be able to read our minds, feel what our hearts feel, and then treat us accordingly. Houston, we have a problem: our hearts can't always be trusted.

Shot Through the Heart

Jeremiah 17:9 reveals that "The heart is deceitful above all things, and desperately sick; who can understand it?" In the ancient world, they didn't view the heart as just a beating organ in the chest. It was the physical and the emotional-intellectual moral center of life. According to *Strong's Concordance*[2], there are 830 Bible verses on the heart (not including an additional 116 on "heart's"). To put that into perspective: Heaven is only mentioned 582 times, sin 448 times, salvation 164 times, and hell 54 times. It stands to reason that the more times something is mentioned in scripture, the more significance we should give to that subject. Side note: God's name is mentioned 4456 times (and as Lord 7838 times), versus man 2617 really should be a red flag that it's all about Him and not just ourselves, but I digress. Interestingly the word "mind" is only mentioned 95 times, implying that we can't think our way to a closer relationship with God. It is easier for us in our intellectual society to have conversations about the inner workings of our minds than it is about our consciousness and the actual content of our hearts.

God emphasizes the self-examination of what is going on in our hearts more than what is going on in our minds. Luke 16:15 states, "You are those who justify yourselves before men, but God knows your hearts. For what is exalted among men is an abomination in the sight of God." Here in the 21st century, we commonly emphasize our outward appearance and the inner workings of our minds over the condition of our hearts. We aren't fooling God. He sees what we have brewing deep within ourselves. (1 Samuel 16:7) He sees the things we keep hidden from our social media accounts and the motives we keep hidden from even the closest of friends. Yet He still loves us unconditionally.

Jesus has a mic drop moment with some Pharisees in Mark 7:21-23 when He says, "For from within, out of the heart of a man come evil thoughts, sexual immorality, theft, murder, adultery, coveting, wickedness, deceit, sensuality, envy, slander, pride foolishness. All these evil things come from within, and they defile a person." Ouch J.C. This is a harsh statement, Rabboni. Way to call out the white elephant in the room. We aren't supposed to talk about these things at dinner parties. That's probably why I don't get invited to too many dinner parties. Unfortunately, these thoughts are all too real inside our hearts, and because of shame, we don't talk about them. We pretend these desires don't exist inside of us until someone else acts a fool, then we pounce at the chance to deflect the attention away from ourselves by calling them out on their shenanigans.

Good begets good, and evil begets evil. Speaking and acting upon the evil thoughts in our hearts is like throwing a stone in a lake and watching the ripple effect. Evil things are becoming increasingly tolerated like they were in the times of the Judges, and it seems as though everyone does what is right in their own eyes. When there is no agreed-upon universal standard of truth, we are left with the choice to view the world through our internal paradigms and then act accordingly.

Paradigms are the installed and learned behaviors, beliefs, and thought patterns that are the unknown powers that create your reality. They are nature versus nurture at its finest (and un-finest at times). It is only when we examine what is truly going on in our hearts that we can make conscious decisions on how to react in situations. When we stop and examine what is going on in our environments and within the deep recesses of our hearts, we can form a battle plan on how to walk

19

more in alignment with God and away from all the grumbling. It's essential to get out of autopilot and to examine what our individual stories entail and what our God-given space in the world encompasses.

Mary, Mary, Quite Contrary... How Does YOUR Garden Grow?

I have many favorite Bible scriptures, but somewhere near the top is Luke 2:19, when "Mary treasured up all these things, pondering them in her heart." This verse takes place right after she had just given birth to Jesus. Within a short time, she had been surprised with a visit from the angel Gabriel, had to tell her fiancé she was pregnant as a virgin (even though everyone in town was probably calling her a ho), traveled all over the place, gave birth in a manger without an epidural, followed with visits from wise men and shepherds she didn't even know. This chick was real Spirit-filled because I would not have reacted so gracefully given the series of events. She was in this moment choosing how to remember her life story: from a glass half full perspective. This inspiring teenage girl's reaction to the chaos is a beautiful example of doing what many fail to do: getting out of autopilot and living fully present in the moment with God. She stopped to take a moment to examine her past and present. She noticed God's divine orchestration of these events and His promise to her fulfilled. She would need to pull these treasured memories of joy out of her heart when she was staring at the mangled body of her beautiful boy on the cross thirty-three years later. It's what we decide to treasure in our hearts that makes us who we are as people and determines how we will interact with the world.

What are you putting into your heart? What are all the things you spend time treasuring up and storing away for later? Back when I was forfeiting my time to endless days of Forensic Files episodes and YouTube sprees on serial killers, some of the nasty treasures to be found in my heart were thoughts about how many hogs it would take to hide the evidence so I wouldn't have to bury a body if the situation were to arise. Not very glorifying to God, and not something I should be pondering in my heart. When someone would piss me off, thoughts of giving them a neck hug for a little too long would spring up from the well within my chest instead of helpful verses like James 1:19-20, Psalm 37:8, or Proverbs 14:29. Don't worry; I've been through therapy and have a sponsor now. As I said, I am intentional about my Jesus and coffee time in the mornings to wrangle my heart into submission.

Sometimes after my quiet time in the mornings, I get the illusion that I am ready to go out into the world as this super saint who will show everyone I interact with that day what walking with Christ looks like. I fantasize about the conversations we will have where they will surely see the angelic glow coming off of my face and then proceed to ask me how I obtained such a beautiful complexion. I will use this opportunity to tell them all about my Jesus, and they will want to follow Him as well. Then I get a message from someone at

4:30 in the morning, right in the middle of my devotional time. I'm not sure when people started thinking it was okay to message anyone that early unless it is an emergency, or you know the person works nights. Just because I am typically up at that ungodly hour does not mean that I am in the mood to be sociable. I happen to be in the middle of trying to socialize with Jesus, asking Him to will into existence my inner Proverbs 31 woman, so my inner Jezebel doesn't come out.

Sayings like, "You are about to watch me go from holy to hood" or "Being a Christian don't make me soft, and the Bible don't make me sweet. I'm from the southside of heaven" resonates with the inner Florida girl within me. Although I look and often act like a blonde valley girl, there is a gangster for God lurking deep within the inner depths of my soul. I can go from being the most Spirit-filled, Jesus-loving woman I know to wanting to rip someone's head off in about 3.5 seconds. It's that whole Mark 7:21-23 thing. My heart clearly still has A LOT of refining to do before it becomes as pure as gold. I need to continue to stay intentional about my heart's treasures.

Basic Instinct

On a more serious note, even with the help of the Holy Spirit dwelling within the hearts of those of us who have asked Him to, our hearts don't always have an accurate discernment of what is right or wrong. We have a natural inclination from an early age to be self-centered, as seen in toddlers when they start to learn how to lie to get what they want. As previously discussed, we have an instinct for domination and manipulating our surroundings for our advantage. When you Google the definition of instinct, it will tell you that it is "an innate, typically fixed pattern of behavior in animals in response to certain stimuli." Biology is hard to change, you filthy animal (said in an Angels With Filthy Souls gangster voice from Home Alone for full effect).

The *Twelve Steps and Twelve Traditions of Alcoholics Anonymous*[3] tell us that creation gave us our instincts for a purpose and that our instincts are necessary and God-given. It also states, "Yet these instincts, so necessary for our existence, often far exceed their proper functions. Powerfully, blindly, many times subtly, they drive us, dominate us, and insist upon ruling our lives. Our desires for sex, for material and emotional security, and for an important place in society often tyrannize us. When thus out of joint, man's natural desires cause him great trouble, practically all the trouble there is. No human being, however good, is exempt from these troubles. Nearly every serious emotional problem can be seen as a case of misdirected instincts. When that happens, our great natural assets, the instincts, have turned into physical and mental liabilities." What stands out to me is that many times it is our basic instincts that are often subconsciously driving us towards our troubles. I listen to numerous preachers on various podcasts, and one of the popular themes here is that "God leads us and the devil drives us."

There is a reason the Bible often compares us to domesticated sheep. (Psalm 23, Mark 6:34, Revelation 7:17, Ezekiel 34:30-31, etc.) These adorable creatures are prone to get lost by wandering off when left to their own devices, and their primary instinct is to follow one another. They have a hard time finding the necessities to survive on their own, and they are relatively defenseless animals that require constant protection from predators. Even though they get a bad rap for being stupid, they are reasonably intelligent animals who have complex social structures within the herd, designating their own kings and leaders to follow, as you might say. Studies have demonstrated that sheep have excellent spatial memory and can memorize and navigate complex mazes months later. They might not be stupid, but they are incredibly strong-willed, stubborn, and want to do things their own way. Sound familiar? To be a successful shepherd, you need a plan and to create a desire within the sheep to go the right way. A wise shepherd will lead from the front, training up an established leader sheep in the flock. The rest of the herd will be directed to green pastures and still waters using their basic instincts.[4]

As Psalm 23 says, the Lord is our Shepherd. He gently goes before us to lead us back to Himself, where we will find true peace and eternal life. However, He gives us free will to decide to follow. Otherwise, it wouldn't be love. God is not a rapist. He will not force

Himself on you. If he did, it would be slavery, not true love. However, He will work on your heart and refine it if you invite Him involuntarily. On the other hand, our enemy satan (intentionally left uncapitalized because I don't respect that fool) often drives us away from God. The psychological definition of drive is "an innate, biologically determined urge to attain a goal or satisfy a need." The enemy uses "our desires for sex, for material and emotional security, and for an important place in society" against us. We all want to feel valued, loved, and secure. When we believe the lie that we can find these things in anything other than God, we start to idolize them in our hearts, and the enemy has the perfect opportunity to drive us away from God so he can eat us for lunch.

We get attacked like this all the time, but we often don't realize what is going on because we are intoxicated with the pursuit of our desires. 1 Peter 5:8 says, "Be sober-minded; be watchful. Your adversary the devil prowls around like a roaring lion, seeking someone to devour." I don't know about you but being eaten alive isn't on my top ten list of ways to die. It's easy to get distracted chasing security and success. We sheeple are built to desire these things. It's also natural to get disgusted and depressed when our domination plans don't work out. That's when our addictions come into play. We try to self-soothe with the medication of our choice (pick your poison: alcohol, drugs, prescription pain killers, food, shopping, sex, social media, perfectionism, etc). Once again, we live in a groaning world, desperately searching for any answer that will provide relief and the secrets to our heart's desires. We switch into autopilot and are driven out of the safety of the green pasture. Then the more our hearts break, and our dreams die. We need a spiritual EKG.

Spiritual EKG

According to *WebMD*, an EKG is "a test that records the electrical activity of your ticker through small electrode patches that a technician attaches to the skin of your chest, arms, and legs."[5] These safe and painless tests check your heart rhythm, blood flow, electrolyte imbalances, and other heart abnormalities. During the test, you lie flat on your back while a computer creates a picture of the electrical impulses that move through your heart.

When you are being tested and tempted, how often do you lie flat on your back in meditation and prayer and ask God to show you where the hurt in your heart is coming from? Not as a passing question, but as an honest open-ended conversation with God where you let Him whisper back to you your life-changing revolutions in the inner recesses of your heart? I can tell you right now that I tend to fall flat on my face before I recognize this as the proper course of action. Our herd encourages loudness and movement, and due to my own past experiences, these quiet moments often make my skin want to crawl. However, as far as I know, all major world religions place significant value on prayer and meditation. There is an underlying awareness across humanity that these two activities are essential for our spiritual well-being.

You might be thinking, "But I try it and don't hear anything." Please don't shoot me for this platitude, but practice makes perfect. Many people talk to God but never hear from Him because they don't know how to listen. Prayer can't be a one-way conversation. It isn't handing over a checklist of our desires or complaining about our life circumstances (although I believe He wants us to have those conversations with Him too). The book *The Practice of the Presence of God* by Brother Lawrence[6] changed my life. Instead of prayers being solely these stoic events at meals and bedtimes, I now think of it as a constant stream of dialogue internally between the creator and me throughout the day. But even with this constant conversation, I sometimes still don't pick up on what He is trying to throw down. That's where meditation comes in. The goal here isn't to empty one's mind like in Eastern meditation, but in a Christian meditation sense where the goal is to ponder Scripture and connect with God (see above example of Mary). It is pondering the promises of God and dwelling upon each and every word. It is where head knowledge is turned into heart knowledge.

Prayer and meditation are God-given tools so we can reconnect with Him in the present moment. Prayer has the power to connect your past to your future. Deuteronomy 4:29-30 promised our ancestors, the Israelite sheeple, in the wilderness that "But from there you will seek the LORD your God and you will find him if you search after him with all your heart and with all your soul. When you are in tribulation, and all these things come upon you in the latter days, you will return to the LORD your God and obey his voice." Keep seeking and you will hear Him. He wants to meet you where you are and show you how your story matters. And your story does matter.

Kintsugi

In the *Gifts of Imperfection: Let Go of Who You Think You're Supposed to Be and Embrace Who You Are* by Brene Brown[7], she points out that "Owning our story can be hard but not nearly as difficult as spending our lives running from it. Embracing our vulnerabilities is risky but not nearly as dangerous as giving up on love and belonging and joy -the experiences that make us the most vulnerable. Only when we are brave enough to explore the darkness will we discover the infinite power of our light."

I love the concept of the Japanese art of kintsugi. This ancient art form is a pottery repair method that honors the pottery's unique history by emphasizing, not hiding, its breaks. The cracks are seamed with resin and precious metals like gold, silver, and platinum. This is what the Potter (Jeremiah 18) is doing with us. When we give our hearts over to Him, He can use our imperfections and heartbreaks to create something more beautiful than what we were before. Believers are seamed with faith, which is more precious than gold, and the result gives praise and glory to God (1 Peter 1:7). Our heartbreaks make us more real to others experiencing their own suffering and looking for healing. When we emerge from the dark places life takes us and share our testimonies of healing on the other side of suffering, people see the light within us and want it too. When we meet people living their best life, it leaves us wanting. We want what they have.

Transparency about our stories is how we connect with others in a meaningful and life-giving way. The following pages are parts of my life story, intermingled directly and indirectly with other people's life stories, with some thought-provoking questions about where we go from here. In the words of Erin Morgenstern, "You may tell a tale that takes up residence in someone's soul, and becomes their blood and self-purpose. That talk will move them and drive them and who knows what they might do because of it, because of your words. That is your role, your gift." Without much ado, here is my story.

ב

Our Childhoods and How They Form Us

"You can accept or reject the way you are treated by other people, but until you heal the wounds of your past, you will continue to bleed"
-Iyanla Vanzant

The name that is on my birth certificate is Tasha Page Johnson. My mother fell in love with the name Natasha from a novel she was reading while she was pregnant with me, and my father vetoed the name because he didn't want to think of a moose every time he called his daughter (here's to you Bullwinkle). They settled on Tasha, which means "Christmas child." I was born in June. This made no sense to me growing up, and to add insult to injury, my father intentionally spelled Page without the "I." The movie *The Pagemaster* came out in the '90s when I was a child, and once the other kids found out that my name wasn't spelled Paige like the pretty girl in class, it was unceasing ridicule for this girl who always had a Goosebumps book in her hand. I had been officially renamed The Pagemaster by my peers, much to my annoyance. Thank God he only gave me boys, so I wasn't tempted to pass the name down to my daughter.

Instead of becoming upset with my peers, I became bitter with my name and my parents, whom I deemed cruel for giving me that name. I held onto that resentment long enough that the first thing I did when I got married was change my middle name to my maiden name. Solved that problem! Little did I know this would not be the conclusion to the story...

I started taking Biblical Hebrew classes with HaSefer Ministries at Baruch HaShem Congregation in 2020 (shameless plug: If you live near San Antonio, go check them out). In that class, my morah (teacher) challenged me to spell my name in Hebrew. One of the things I love most about Hebrew is that each letter of the Aleph-Bet has a pictorial meaning, which gives words a more profound interpretation. There are two letters for "T": ט and ת. The pictorial meaning for ט is "snake," and ת is "covenant." I didn't want the snake one, so I chose to spell my name תאשה which would make my name meaning, "To reveal a consuming covenant." Since I'm in a covenant relationship with Christ, I considered this a personalized hug from God that He loves me, and there was indeed a deeper purpose to my name. My name wasn't an accident, and that the Christmas child born in June was intentionally named with purpose from the beginning. I wore my name as a badge of honor and with new pride. God's sense of humor never ceases to amaze me. To keep me from becoming too proud, I learned a year later in a modern Hebrew class I had to use the ט spelling since the ת spelling creates the "Th" sound. My name isn't "Thasha", although the thought of changing my name once again did cross through my mind. So טאשה, the revealer of consuming snakes it is. Just so you don't say I didn't live up to my name, I should tell you that you should know there is a consuming snake introduced to us in Genesis 3 that is still trying to consume all of us at this very moment. Run Forrest, run!

We can't run from our destinies. A good starting point for finding your destiny might be in examining your name. The Bible has example after example of individuals who lived up to their names.[1] Abraham, the "father of many," is the paternal figure for the three major world religions. The name of his grandson Jacob means "supplanter" (accurate), which was changed to Israel (meaning "he who wrestles with God") after he wrestled with the angel of the Lord. Throughout the Old Testament, we see the Israelites wrestle with God repeatedly in the wilderness so that this name would seem accurate for God's chosen people. Satan translates to "adversary," which many of God's children can attest is accurate as we go to war with him daily.

The name above all names (Philippians 2:9-11), ישוע Yeshua, or Jesus as we know Him, translates to "salvation." Dave Adamson[2] points out in his book that when Jesus went to the house of Zacchaeus and said, "Today salvation has come to this house," that he was making a pun because that is what Jesus came to earth to do, and it was also his name's meaning. Who said God isn't a funny guy? I mean, the guy clearly has a sense of humor. Look at the platypus. The meaning of Yeshua's name gives a deeper significance to verses like Isaiah 12:2: "Surely God is my salvation."

What does your name mean? Even if it means "swine" like Portia or "ugly head" like Kennedy, the definition might not be why you were given that name. There are no accidents in God's kingdom. Sue discovered in good ole Johnny Cash's classic hit *A Boy Named Sue* that his name wasn't a cruel mistake after all. His father saw the bigger picture. He gave him the name Sue to make him tough enough to survive a cruel world fatherless since he knew he wouldn't be able to be there for him. He walked away from that conversation with a few bruises and a greater appreciation for his name. Your future depends on how you choose to remember your past. Like a trapeze artist, you can't hold on to the past, but you can use it to launch you into your future destiny.

What You Don't Work Out, You Will Act Out

We can't hold onto the past, but we do need to be aware of the content of our stories so we can live intentionally about finding our authentic selves and our God-given space in the world. According to *Strong's Concordance*[3], the word "Behold" is mentioned in the Bible 1327 times, which suggests its importance. Behold means "to see or observe." Human consciousness can be a blessing and a curse. We hold on to everything from our pasts when often we just need to let go and *be held* by the one who will love us unconditionally. At the end of the day, that's what we are all genuinely searching for more than anything else: unconditional love. When we wish our pasts were different, it forms resentments within us. Resentments are deadly roots in our hearts that devour and destroy us. (Hebrews 12:15) When we choose not to forgive ourselves and others, it means we are choosing to continue suffering. Unacceptance of reality causes suffering.

From the book *Picture Perfect*[4], Amy Baker notes, "Humans are complex creatures. All who belong to the Lord are a mixture of saint, sufferer, and sinner." Every person you will ever meet is a mixture of these three characteristics. When we resort to black and white judgmental thinking, we stereotype others and dehumanize them. The world and the people in it are complex, uncertain, and constantly changing. Serial killers and pedophiles didn't become the monsters we perceive them to be overnight. They are products of their environments: and the interactions with those people, places, and things. The character of a person is formed by millions of small decisions made over a lifetime. Taking time to examine the good, the bad, and the ugly from our pasts, and within ourselves, is important because you need to know what *your* character's prototype is. This way you can change out dysfunctional parts and recalculate your flight path if you don't like the trajectory you are headed towards.

One of my favorite metaphors is that maneuvering through life peacefully can be compared to the body mechanics of a bird. A bird needs two wings to fly, just as we need equal parts of God's grace and truth. If we have all truth and no grace, we have a broken wing, and we can't fly without the Spirit's help towards our purpose. The reverse is true as well. To soar like eagles and not grow weary, (Isaiah 40:31) we need to look at our pasts with grace and truth. This way, we don't beat ourselves up, but we can learn to love ourselves as we repent and grow. Until we do the hard work of digging deep and pulling the resentments out of our hearts, we will continue to suffer and inflict pain on those around us. The problem starts within the heart. Chasing happiness or changing environments won't fix things for long. As the saying goes, "wherever you go, there you are."

What's Love Got to Do with It?

We can't truly love others until we learn to love ourselves, and none of us want to end up on our deathbed with a life full of regrets from not living our best life. When we are raised in homes without equal parts grace and truth, all kinds of things go haywire. The fact is, *none* of us were raised in homes with equal parts grace and truth because we were all raised by humans. Ian Israel[5] notes in his book *How to Survive Your Childhood Now That You're an Adult*, "To release our resentment about not being loved unconditionally, the greatest tool we can use is to forgive everyone equivocally. Our parents and teachers and siblings and relatives and friends did the best they could with the tools they had at the time, so we must forgive them.

Period. Unforgiveness manifests as resentment or absurdly wanting things we cannot change to change."

My father was an Air Force brat raised by a very authoritative, and at times abusive, man. As a member of the 1960's counterculture, my long-haired father naturally butted heads with my strict military grandfather. To this day, Dad still wears flip-flops everywhere, and he lovingly reminded me on my 30th birthday that I was no longer trustworthy. He's hilarious. I inherited his love for flip-flops as well as his dry sense of humor, above-average intelligence, affection for science, drive to learn, and hippie spirit. Although he will argue he was a "freak" and not a hippie because he's still into that whole bucking the system thing.

Having children is a beautiful thing, and most of us set out to do this parenting thing right. We tend to look at how we were raised and use that as a baseboard to raise our own children. We look at the pros and cons and decide what we will take with us in our own parenting journeys to influence our children. In the 1960s, a psychologist named Diana Baumrind developed her Pillar Theory on parenting styles, with two other researchers Maccoby and Martin refining it in the 1980s. According to their revisions on the theory, there are four parenting styles: Authoritative, Authoritarian (or Disciplinarian), Permissive (or Indulgent), and Neglectful (or Uninvolved).[6] I could: A) spend four paragraphs explaining their work, or B) you could Google it for a much clearer explanation. Let's go with plan B so I don't get squirreled again.

My hippie father seemingly disagreed with many aspects of his authoritarian upbringing because he tended to parent more permissively in some areas when it came time to parent my brother and me. When I approached my teenage years and started exhibiting sexual promiscuity and substance abuse issues, he permitted (and at times even applauded) my behavior instead of disciplining me. At times he acted more like a friend, but whenever I pushed too far, the authoritarian upbringing he was raised with would come out. I am so proud of him for breaking the cycle of physical abuse, but the remnants of the emotional abuse he was raised with would appear like a splinter festering from time to time when my actions didn't agree with his world paradigm. He would alternate between yelling at us with a deep booming voice and stonewalling us with silence.

Even though I knew without a doubt he loved me, I still always felt like I walked on eggshells and needed to try harder to be perfect. It also subconsciously altered my view of God, because we tend to form our initial view of our heavenly Father based on our relationship with our earthly fathers (and mothers). For the most part, growing up I viewed God as a loving friend, but one with only a limited amount of patience for my failures and imperfections. I was always waiting for him to lash out at me when He hit His limit, or to stonewall me with crippling silence when I failed to perform the part I was expected to play without a script to read from. Discerning the truth of my past is the key to success for my future. I had to let any resentments go and acknowledge the past for what it was: the foundation that made me. Regardless of anything that's happened, I know I am one of the lucky ones because I grew up loved by my family. Even though we have our flaws, I have a fantastic family. My little brother and his beautiful wife finally got around to giving my boys some cousins, and I look forward to watching how they raise their two beautiful children. At least they had a little girl, so I can finally buy some pink stuff! Even though my brother and I have the same parents, we have turned out different in many ways. He works with politicians and I am a religious freak, so we are a lot of fun during dinner parties. All joking aside, no matter our differences, I love him very much.

Six Hour Standoff

As I will talk about in chapter 3, I am a sexual assault survivor. I held these secrets inside for years after the abuse. To be honest, I'm not entirely sure why I didn't feel secure enough to tell my parents right after these events transpired. Perhaps it was because I knew what had happened was terrible, and my distorted childlike logic thought this made me terrible too. I felt dirty, and I wanted them to think of me as a good girl. "Good girls" keep their dresses blemish free. It seemed more logical to hold the painful secrets inside at the time because I didn't want to burden them with any more problems since they were distracted with their marriage falling apart and financial troubles. Whatever the reasons for my silence may be, I have had this overwhelming feeling that I am not secure in the world from an early age. Since I am not safe, I subconsciously think if I try harder and strive more, then I can prevent bad things from happening to me since nobody else will protect me. This false fear-based narrative from the enemy has wrecked all kinds of havoc in my life and my relationships with others, especially God.

Although I did for years, I no longer harbor bitterness in my soul towards my parents about the past. They did the best they could with the tools they had from their upbringing. When we don't forgive others, it's like drinking poison and expecting them to get sick. We all want to feel valued, loved, and appreciated. We were all denied these opportunities in one way or another as children. Therefore, we all developed unique styles of interacting with the world to seek this love we have been looking for our whole lives. The love we pursue isn't a feeling: it is a person, and He died for you on Calvary.

Based on your upbringing, you might cringe when you hear that. I wouldn't blame you because Christians can suck at times. It's been a raw spot in my relationship with my father because at the time I am writing this, he still does not have a personal relationship with Jesus Christ. Christ is the center of my world, so it sometimes leads to awkward conversations because our paradigms are so different.

My Texan grandmother was raised Southern Baptist, and she was going to be damned if her son wasn't baptized. So, my father was baptized: after a six-hour standoff where they told him he wasn't leaving that tub until he agreed to accept Jesus into his heart and get dunked. Being from a small town where everybody talked, I'm assuming the decisions she made were out of fear of being judged as a bad parent. I don't blame my father for having some severe resentments with Christ, and his followers, after what he went through growing up. When we don't act in love, we push others away from God. The cycle of pain continued one small decision at a time.

A relationship with Christ should never be forced. True Christianity isn't about rules or impressing our neighbors with our holiness. It's a personal relationship with Jesus. The only one in the universe who has the right to throw stones at you has never picked up a stone to hurl at you when you have missed the mark of perfection. (John 8:1-11) Instead, He laid His life down as a sacrifice so that you could spend an eternity with Him because our sins separate us from Him. After all, He is a holy God. He is a God of grace and truth. His life always showed both of these two characteristics, even as He put the needs of others around him first while he was dying the most agonizing death on the cross. (Luke 23:43 and John 19:26)

God isn't afraid of being vulnerable with us. He sent us His heart in the flesh to show us the way back to Him. He has the perfect heart of a father and doesn't make mistakes like our earthly fathers do. He knows that we aren't perfect, but this doesn't stop Him from giving us what we need out of His grace. When we can't see His hand in the circumstances of our lives, we have to trust His heart in faith. He loves us, and He is love. (1 John 4:7-21) We love because He first loved us.

Amazing Grace: How Sweet the Home

I'm currently trying to raise my boys in a home filled with grace and truth, hoping they will internalize the concept that they are loved unconditionally regardless of their actions. I look forward to reading the books they will write after they have gone through years of expensive therapy sessions due to my parenting mistakes. I wasn't as loving towards their half-sister when she was under my care, and the fruit of that is apparent in the life of emotional turmoil she is living out now as a young adult. CPS removed her from her drug-addicted mother when she was 4, and we were granted full custody shortly after I turned 20. She was developmentally behind in almost all areas of life and required physical therapy, speech therapy, sensory therapy, and weekly visits with a childhood psychologist. At the time, I was enrolled in college full time, worked a work-study position part-time, was president of Psychology Club, and ran the household by myself because her father worked out of state on wind turbines/ cell phone towers. To say I was young and overwhelmed is an understatement. I don't know how to juggle this many things without feeling a crippling amount of pressure.

Although functional from outward appearances, I was debilitated by a painful struggle with endometriosis and consequential painkiller addiction, which left me impaired in many ways. I was very harsh and, at times, emotionally abusive with her because I couldn't handle my own emotions and love her in a selfless grace-based parenting style. Years later, after I got sober and could see the inappropriate patterns in my parenting, I had to ask her forgiveness and continue trying to make living amends and be more loving in the future. I also had to forgive myself for the cruel ways I treated her because there is no personal growth in the shame pit. I was doing my best with the tools I had at the time. My heart needed a major overhaul and I needed better coping tools. I was doing my best.

Dr. Tim Kimmel's book *Grace Based Parenting*[7] is an excellent resource for those looking to raise children in homes with grace and truth. For many, the concept of truth comes easier, but what does a grace-based home look like and why is this important? Grace from a Christian perspective is "unmerited favor." We all mess up and are deserving of judgment. Judgment kills. Only grace makes us alive. You can't have grace when you have rules and little relationship. "Grace based homes are a vital link to children's wholeness and wellbeing as adults. That's because our vulnerabilities have the power to define us if we aren't careful. Legalism, student or rigid parenting models and preoccupied moms and dads can keep children from growing beyond their vulnerabilities. Grace is the key that unlocks the door to a balanced life."

It's a delicate balancing act. Relationships without rules don't result in grace either. Children need rules without feeling like their identities are being judged. My mother always used to tell me, "I might not love your actions, but I will always love you." This is the perfect example of grace and truth in my opinion. She was letting me know that my identity wasn't found in what I do. I know now it is found in who I am because of Christ. (Galatians 2:20 and 2 Corinthians 5:17) My decisions may shape the trajectory of my life, but they will never form my identity.

Hiding in the Baggage

In the book of 1 Samuel, the Israelites demand a King to rule over them like the other nations. God warns them it's a bad idea because Israel was meant to be set apart from the other nations because they were God's chosen people. However, they wouldn't listen, so the Lord directs Samuel to appoint Saul king. He fit the appearance of what a king should look like on the outside. However, we can see heart issues on the inside of Saul from the very beginning.

Samuel gathered all of the tribes of Israel to present their new king to the kingdom. The problem was, Saul was nowhere to be found. The Lord had to tell the people, "Behold, he is hiding himself by the baggage." (1 Samuel 10:22) I suffer from anxiety and insecurity as well, so I can relate to his reaction. My perfectionism tendencies instilled in my childhood rear their ugly head from time to time, and I shut down when I feel I'm at risk of people judging me. Heaven forbid someone on earth doesn't like me! Instead of focusing on the people God has placed in my life that do love me, and more importantly, the love God has for me, I hide. Or I fixate and become obsessed with fixing the perceived problem myself instead of handing my troubles over to the one who holds all the answers.

Saul's addiction to earning the approval of fellow man above God eventually led him to be disobedient to God's commands. Therefore, he sacrificed God's best plan for his life. The kingdom was torn from him. Sin cuts out God's favor in our lives, but it never cuts out his love for us. He is always looking for a willing soul to fight kingdom battles, but he won't give us the blessings we crave if our hearts are in the wrong place because we aren't equipped to handle them once we get them. This is seen in the life of Saul, as he was more concerned with impressing the people than serving God. Pride comes before the fall. I also fell hard, so I can relate to tall Saul.

The Lord picks David to be Saul's replacement. We are told that he is picked because of his heart, not his outward appearance like Saul. His family didn't value him enough to bring him to the lineup when his father Jesse was told to round up all of his sons. Ouch. Instead, they left him in the field tending to the sheep. The Lord directs Samuel to David, and he anoints him. From outward appearances, his life circumstances don't change overnight, and he isn't magically taken to the palace like Cinderella. He is, however, filled with the Holy Spirit from that moment on. When we surrender our lives over to the Holy Spirit, he will slowly direct our steps towards God's true calling on our life. When we stay obedient to his Word, we will see our hearts change, and God's favor in our lives increase over time.

Making this commitment to Christ doesn't always mean we will earn favor with our families and the people in our lives though. A short while later, 1 Samuel 17 that David's father Jesse still doesn't see him as the king he will be because he still sends him out to bring supplies to his brothers on the front line. Saul is still king at this time, and is still hiding in the metaphorical baggage. As a giant himself, he is the only one big enough to fight Goliath, but he is too insecure and terrified to step on the battlefield. Forty days drag on, and David enters on the scene. We see in verse 22 that he drops the cargo off with a luggage keeper and enters to greet his brothers. I love the stark difference between the two kings here. One hides in the baggage of his insecurities and the other discards his. We can't bring the emotional baggage from our pasts into our future battles. This is why forgiveness is key. Resentments will weigh you down. Our families may never treat us with love and kindness, but when we are filled with the Spirit, we don't need the approval of others to move forward.

Not everyone will be happy to see forward movement in your life when the chains of your past are being broken. Eliab, David's oldest brother, burned with envy and criticized him when he started questioning why this Philistine was taunting the armies of the living God. Instead of letting this stop him, David turned away and talked to other people. Like a plant that has outgrown its pot, sometimes we need to replant ourselves around other supportive people outside of the family systems we grew up in. We saw in the passage above that there was a designated baggage keeper. Don't hold your baggage inside. Find someone qualified to help you sort through what is worth keeping and what needs to go. If you struggle with toxicity from your history, there is no shame in seeking professional help. You can't see the forest through the trees, and having a birds-eye view of our paradigms can help us work on what needs to be changed.

What works for one person might not work for another. There isn't one path to healing. Saul offered David his armor, but it wasn't a good fit for him and would have weighed him down. He needed to examine his past and utilize the strengths from it to fight his giant. The giants in our lives aren't going away. We can choose to hide in our addictions and baggage like Saul. We can choose to ignore the problem and live on autopilot like the Israelites. Or we can drop the baggage, and run towards our destinies like David. The Messiah descended from the line of David. You never know how the world will be impacted by your courage and willingness to change what needs to be changed.

Brick Houses and Wolves

What did your household look like growing up? Did you live in a home that prioritized both grace and truth? Did the house that built you leave you more traumatized than gratified? We have to examine our personal history to know who we are. The good news is that if you don't know who you are, you can become whoever God wants you to be. If we grew up in houses made of sticks and straw and our world seems to be crumbling because the wolves in our lives are blowing us around, then we can scramble away as fast as we can to the safety of our brother's house. He is the Cornerstone, (Isaiah 28:16, 1 Peter 2:4-9) and there is safety for all who place their faith in Him.

The wolf can chase you down the lane, and at times it will feel like you have been caught. Those experiences are frightening because we have an enemy seeking to eat your lunch. (1 Peter 5:8) This is why it is essential to stay sober-minded so you can run with endurance to the hill where your help comes from. (Psalm 121:1) Those in the household of Christ know the battle has already been won. The enemy can huff and puff all he wants to. In the end, just when he thinks he will climb down the chimney to get us, he will fall into the boiling pot to be tormented forever and ever. (Revelation 20:10)

The future may be sealed for the enemy, but it's not for you. If we change our narrative, we change our lives. The Bible teaches us repeatedly through the examples of the lives included within the pages that our beginnings should never be held against us. We have the power each day to take one step at a time towards fully living by surrendering and dying to ourselves a little more.

ג

Innocence Lost

"The initial trauma of a young child may go
underground but it will return to haunt us"
- James Garbarino

One of the enemy's most effective tools in his
arsenal is trying to get us to forget. If he can get us
to forget whose child we are, we forget our identities
and are lost. (John 1:12) If we forget the goodness the
Lord has already done in our life, we become
discouraged and feel abandoned. (Joshua 12:14) If we
forget where our help comes from, we will become lost
and afraid. (Psalm 121:1-2) If we forget our freedom
was given on Calvary, we stay enslaved to the sins that
chain us. (Romans 6:17-19) If we forget who God is, we
forget how to truly love. (1 John 4:16) Satan is
constantly attacking the truth because he is the father
of lies, (John 8:44) and he is trying to separate us from
God permanently.

Our stories hold power. Satan wants us to forget
them. How you choose to remember the past holds
power to change your future by changing your
thoughts and how you approach life. Remembering the
details is sometimes painful. Only sadists get pleasure
from pain, and most of us aren't sadists. If you are a

sadist, I'm surprised that you made it this far into this book. That must have been painful, so I don't know whether to congratulate you or be concerned because the pain brought you joy. You might ought to think about therapy. In all honesty, we all could use therapy. No shame, my friend. We're all doing our best.

Moving right along, most of us tend to avoid the things that hurt us. There are a million ways the enemy can drive us towards trying to forget our past: condemnation, keeping us overly busy, messing with our brain/body chemistry/hormones, substance abuse/addictions, etc. However, the truth remains tucked inside of us though, even if we repress it.

I pursued a degree in psychology because I was sick of being in pain and thought if I went down that career track that I would have an insider view of how the human mind worked so I could prevent people from hurting me anymore. That, and I had a tarot card reader in New Orleans tell me at 14 that I would grow up to be a lawyer with four kids and divorced by 35, so I switched my planned career path to avoid that fate. Don't mess with tarot cards kids. We can't see the spiritual warfare behind the scenes, so that's not a playground we should play on. Any rate, I learned that a psychology degree does not give you magical powers that leave you impenetrable to the wrath of others. I also learned about the psychological concept of repression during that time.

Repression, from a psychological perspective, is when we unconsciously block unpleasant emotions, impulses, memories, and thoughts from our conscious minds.[1] The purpose of this is to minimize pain, guilt, and anxiety. When we do this, it divides us from our true selves and the forgiveness we were meant to give.

What memories are you repressing? You might be asking yourself, "Why on earth would I want to recall these things? If I wanted them, I probably wouldn't have blocked them in the first place!" From the documentary Cracked Up[2] based on the autobiography "God If You're Not Up There I'm F*****"[3] by SNL's Darrell Hammond, "When people are behaving in apparently self-destructive ways, it's time to stop asking what's wrong with them, and time to start asking what happened to them."

The Secret Closet

Years after the fact, I recovered the memory of my babysitter molesting me when I was about five or six. My mom had asked a teenage boy from church to babysit my brother and me. He would make us play hide and seek, but he would never seem to find my brother. Instead, he would make me perform oral sex on him. He told me that this "game" was a secret and that my parents didn't need to know about it. This is yet another example that the church is actually more like a hospital with sick people than a museum full of saints. It wasn't until years later when I was a suicidal addict in therapy when we were trying to examine how

I ended up in that chair, that I remembered all these details. That small rock thrown into the pond of my life created a ripple that had devastating consequences.

What my five or six-year-old brain took from this event (and others) was that I needed to live to please other people, even at the expense of my personal comfort. My body was an object, to be used for the pleasure of other people. I wasn't secure in the world and my parents wouldn't protect me. My thirty-four-year-old brain now knows that my mom didn't intentionally drop the ball when she chose him to watch me. She thought she was making an excellent choice in a babysitter because who expects the family friend's son from church to be a teenage child molester?

Hurt people hurt people. I could have spent the rest of my life angry at him for taking advantage of me, but that wouldn't be productive. I have no idea what he has been through, and what kinds of demons he has battled. I have to look at him from a hurt human perspective instead of a monster, and I have to forgive him. Not because he deserves it, because what he did was deplorable. But because I need to for my own freedom. I can't carry that rock of resentment in my heart because it will drown me if I do, as I have seen it do in my past. He is running around out there somewhere in the world, probably unaware of the pain he caused me. What sense would it make to continue to let him hurt me over and over again daily by continuing to stay mad?

We are commanded to love our neighbors as ourselves. (Mark 12:31, Leviticus 19:18, Matthew 22:36-40) I have made my own mistakes throughout life and hurt others deeply. I might not have murdered anyone or molested a child, but if I had followed the example of the world, it could have easily swung that way (see the section in chapter 1 on burying bodies and neck hugs). I would be a pharisee to think that I'm better than anyone else because I'm not. That would be prideful, and pride is at the center of an evil heart. Remember Jeremiah 17:9? As long as we continue to have this "us" versus "them" mentality towards people who commit horrific crimes, we dehumanize them and segregate a whole section of the human population who needs our help the most.

This is not to say that there shouldn't be consequences for their actions, because there absolutely should. Serial killers and child molesters should not be roaming the streets with the opportunity to commit future crimes unless they have been completely rehabilitated and served their time. Forgiveness does not always mean reconciliation. But let's put down the fire and pitchforks, and be less like the Pharisees. I realize I won't be popular for saying any of this. But we can't continue to accept a watered-down, prosperity gospel that is convenient for us. We, as Christian's can't pick and choose what parts of the Bible we will accept and what neighbors we will choose to love. We have to forgive everyone. Even those who hurt us the deepest and stole our innocence. Let's get them therapy and support groups as we do for alcoholics and drug addicts. Let's stop labeling them as monsters deserving of death and start looking at them as sick people who need help. Let's break the generational cycle of abuse. Let's stop hurting ourselves by filling our hearts with hate.

If this section is filling you with rage, stop and ask yourself where the anger is stemming from. Do you have repressed memories or unresolved trauma from your past that is boiling within? Are you dealing with shame from an act you might have committed? There is no shame at the foot of the cross. The human sex drive is one of the strongest impulses within the human body. Left unchecked, our impulses drive us into making mistakes and inflicting pain on others. It takes great strength to resist compulsions, as any addict will tell you. Addictions are too powerful for most of us to resist on our own. That's why most recovery programs require you to turn the problem over to a higher power of your choosing. Don't be fooled: we are all addicted to something. Your addiction might be more socially acceptable and less destructive, but it's still slowly killing you.

Fear is also one of humankind's strongest impulses. Fear drives us to be unloving towards others and to make destructive decisions. It takes great strength to run towards the things that make us afraid. What would it say to the world if we were to run towards forgiveness? A person who has been shown grace is much more likely to repent and help others than someone outcasted in hate. Let's stop looking at people in splitting (all or nothing) thinking and try to see our own monsters as children loved by God instead. After all, someone out there might think you are a monster too. Love conquers all things.

Doe, A Deer, A Female Deer

Speaking of splitting thinking, my personality is a mix of juicy contradictions. I am a bougie hippie redneck. I'm a book-loving nerd who loves rap (well, all music really). I'm a girly girl that will get down and dirty in the mud (in a tutu). I'm in recovery from addiction and alcoholism, yet I still go to bars and dance with friends. Although I do admit, I dance like a stereotypical white girl. I take Hebrew at a messianic synagogue, and I go to a nondenominational Christian church (shout out Community Bible Church in San Antonio). I'm on a no beef/pork/gluten/ dairy diet, yet (at the risk of losing my PETA readers) I have to admit I am an avid hunter.

I started hunting in my mid-twenties and fell in love with everything about it: the feeling of having a full freezer, knowing that the meat is organic and healthy, the adventure of the hunt and the stories to be shared with other hunters (like the time I shot an 11-foot alligator and found out I was pregnant when I went to cook the meat and got nauseous as only a preggo does). I love having the animals mounted on my wall, bedazzled with tiaras and other jewelry. Most of all, I love being alone with God outdoors and watching the majesty of all He has created. Even a "bad" day hunting is a fantastic day. I love watching the animals, especially deer. They are by far my favorite animal.

Deer are modest, shy, and rather timid animals. They have an excellent sense of discernment and are always on the alert. Deer are typically very good at smelling danger and running away from it in time. We also know from the common idiom that they tend to get "caught" in headlights. When their eyes are suddenly struck by the beam of a car's headlights, its fully dilated pupils become blinded by the abundance of light, so it cannot see at all. Not knowing what to do, a deer will stand still and wait for its eyes to adjust to the blinding light. It's part of the deer's defense circuitry designed to scan for sensory information of incoming signs of danger, and once an attack is detected dominates its brain functioning. So, it freezes.[4]

Humans have three typical responses to incoming danger: flight, fight, or freeze. This isn't a conscious response. Instead, it's an automatic response controlled by the autonomic nervous system (ANS). Your specific physiological reactions depend on how you usually respond to stress. We train our military and first responders to override their bodies' natural flight and fear mechanisms by repetitive exposure to stressful situations. This way, when danger threatens, their muscle memory will kick in and they will react in self-defense or other problem-solving ways. However, most sexual assault survivors have not been trained in this way. Psychotherapist Noel McDermott[5] says that freezing is a much more common response to terror, like being raped, than fight or flight is. Also, being the hormonally controlled creatures that we are, a prior response to a terrifying situation does not always result in someone responding that way in all future situations as well.

I was fourteen when I entered high school and met a guy I will refer to as Amnon so that I don't use his real name. I was still a virgin, although I had sexually experimented with two neighborhood boys by this point. I was 6'0 and looked like a walking stick at 120 pounds. I was a gangly girl who didn't look like my gorgeous well-endowed girlfriends in the areas that mattered most to teenage boys. So, when a 6'4 neighborhood boy took notice of me, I was ecstatic. My divorced single mother worked for CPS, and her work schedule was erratic, so I didn't always have supervision in the evenings.

I snuck out of the house to meet Amnon and had assumed it would be more of the same. I tend to be naive and assume that people are as kind-hearted as I try to be, which isn't always the case. We went to his house and started making out. As things progressed, I realized he wanted to go all the way, which I hadn't done before, so I asked him to stop. He wasn't taking no for an answer, calling me a dick tease, and I physically froze when he started to get rough. I remember that he wasn't listening to any of my requests to stop, and I could not muster up enough willpower to fight to get him off of me. After he had finished, he threw my pants at me as I was bawling, and told me to get out and walk home by myself. I knew deep within that wasn't the way losing your virginity was supposed to look. At the time, I didn't know to classify this as an unacknowledged rape because the rape scripts I had always seen on TV involved a stranger jumping out from the bushes or a stranger at the bar using a date rape drug. I knew nothing about the freeze response to trauma, and I assumed the problem was me because I didn't fight with everything I had to get him to stop.

I became incredibly withdrawn and depressed. My situation became even worse when Amnon went around the neighborhood and school telling everyone that I was a slut, and that I was horrible in bed. He told everyone that having sex with me was like "f*cking a floppy fish." I couldn't go to my parents about it because my mom worked for CPS in the state of Florida for crying out loud. And I had snuck out of the house, so I wrongfully assumed that they would say I deserved it. I became suicidal and my drug usage increased. My fourteen-year-old brain could not make sense of all that had taken place.

Personal Jesus

In the middle of all this pain, I met a boy we will call Depeche. He was fighting his own demons, but he was kind and compassionate in a seemingly cruel and hopeless world. Once he found out about what happened he went on a mission to beat up Amnon and restore my honor. Except that he lost that fistfight, which just made the ridicule that much worse at school. Looking back, this was the beginning of my tendency to look for security in romantic partners, most of whom were incapable of giving it to me because true security is found in God alone. We can't all have our own personal "Jesus" because that person would be a false idol. But Jesus can be personally ours, and He seeks a relationship with all of us.

My mom got me into therapy a year or two later because my drug usage and suicidal ideation had increased exponentially by the time we moved to Minnesota. This is where I came to terms with understanding that what had happened was rape. However, I quickly learned while talking with peers and new potential partners that most people do not consider it rape unless there was a dramatic fight scene and you did your best to claw their eyes out. The freeze response isn't commonly understood, and one of the biggest rape myths is that not fighting back is an indication of consent.

So due to a lack of compassion or empathy, I quickly realized that I would need to change the story to what my response to the rape was to avoid being blamed or told that it wasn't rape. I learned that if I told people that I fought back, they would respond more appropriately, with more empathy instead of acting like the Spanish Inquisition. The discrepancy in the truth and my modified version of what I thought people wanted to hear created shame because my life story wasn't authentic when I told it. Only truth satisfies the soul.

As the years passed, I learned lesson after lesson with men that my body was viewed as a sexual object, and I eventually figured out I could use that to my advantage. I became manipulative and used men to get what I wanted instead of being the victim all the time. This helped to add to the ever-increasing list of reasons I felt I needed to self-medicate the profound pain inside of my heart. The incident with Amnon started a ripple effect of adverse events that would get worse year after year until Jesus hit me in the head with a two-by-four in rehab and got my attention. More on that in the next chapter.

When the Thunder Rolls

The word "climatized" means to acclimate to a new environment.[6] It is typically used regarding how we respond to weather conditions, but I would argue that it could be used in all areas of life. Judith Lewis Herman reminds us that "Recovery unfolds in three stages. The central task of the first stage is the establishment of safety. The central task of the second stage is remembrance and mourning. The central focus of the third stage is reconnection with ordinary life."[7]

Recovery from sexual assault can be compared to surviving a storm. If you, or someone you know, is currently being sexually abused, know that there is help out there no matter what the perpetrator says.

Help is available. At the time I'm writing this book, the number to the National Sexual Assault Hotline is 1-800-656-4673.[8] Tell a parent, law enforcement officer, teacher, friend, coworker, someone, anyone. Even if the first person you tell doesn't respond appropriately or with compassion, that doesn't mean you should stop trying. You don't deserve what happened to you, and I beg you to reach out to a lifeline and get out of the floodwaters. Keeping trauma inside our hearts eventually drowns us.

After you are in a safe place and no longer at risk for the abuse to continue, please seek professional help dealing with what has happened. Whether that be a professional counselor or a support group, we mustn't minimize or repress the hurts inflicted upon us. Grieving or mourning is a natural response to sexual trauma. Loss of innocence, loss of feeling safe, loss of trust and security are all common losses experienced by survivors. Whenever we experience loss of any kind, we can't stuff it away or fast forward through it, or it will come back to haunt us later. What we don't work out, we will act out. You don't have to work this out alone.

Finally, know that there is life out there after the storm. Immediately after I was raped, it felt like the whole world continued on, and didn't care that it felt like my heart had been ripped out. A hurricane wrecked my world, and I didn't want to go on because it seemed the destruction was too great. Holocaust survivor Viktor E. Frankl saw and experienced unimaginable destruction in ways that most of us will hopefully never experience in this lifetime. In his book *Man's Search for Meaning*, he reminds us that "Everything can be taken from a man but one thing: the last of the human freedoms- to choose one's attitude in any given set of circumstances, to choose one's own way."[9]

I could have chosen to stay angry and hateful forever. But that would have killed me. Hate is a prolonged form of suicide. Once I chose to stop hiding the pain that was buried in my heart and surrender it to God, he was able to heal the hurting parts. As I write this, He's still healing my heart and my defective thought patterns that stem from my childhood trauma. I know that this pain was never His will for my life, but I can use my pain to be vulnerable with others who have experienced the same pain. It's a thorn that keeps me humble and allows me to find my God-given space in the world to connect with others. I can use this thorn to love God more and to love others. If I could say anything to Amnon right now, I would say Genesis 50:20 "As for you, you meant evil against me, but God meant it for good, to bring it about that many people should be kept alive, as they are today." The enemy has already stolen enough. I'm taking my power back and using this evil for good.

מזל טוב

Congratulations! You made it to the end of chapter 3. I promised way back in chapter 1 that if you made it to the end of this chapter that my comment on serial killers and pedophiles doing their personal best would make a little more sense. We are all a mess, some of us more than others. You might still want to tar and feather me for saying that, and depending on your past hurts I wouldn't blame you. I'm just grateful you hung in there and are still reading. You are stronger than you think. You are strong enough to get out of autopilot and to examine what makes you *you*. I challenge you to make it to the end of the book now. Check your seatbelt because chapter 4 covers some pretty serious subject matter. Buckle up, buttercup!

7

Fun Times Or
Dirty Lies?

"Thus says the LORD:
Stand by the roads, and look,
and ask for the ancient paths,
Where the good way is; and walk in it,
and find rest for your souls.
But they said, 'We will not walk in it'"
-Jeremiah 6:16

There is no pulling the wool over God's eyes. He knows what's going on inside of us even before we do. What He saw in Noah's day broke his heart. We are told that the wickedness of man was great and every intention of the heart was evil continually. He couldn't bear it anymore. He decided He would push the reset button and flood the earth. "But Noah found favor in the eyes of the LORD." (Genesis 6:8) We are also told he was a righteous man, blameless for his time, and that he walked with God. Because the Lord finds favor with Noah, He handpicks him for a colossal construction project: to build a boat big enough to save his family and a male/ female pair of every kind of animal. He completes the work, and the fruit of his obedience is that every living thing on the boat is spared as the Lord cleanses the world and establishes His covenant with him and his descendants.

(Genesis 9:9) And then he goes off happily ever after, smiling at the rainbows and walking humbly with God all the days of his life. Yeah, no. Not exactly.

We are told one of the first things that Noah does when he steps out of the boat is to plant a vineyard, farm it, and then get white girl wasted. I'm surprised he wasn't drinking tequila because not only did he get completely hammered, the wine made his clothes fall off. Will Ferrell must be his spirit animal. Either way, Mr. Righteous seems to forget all of the miracles he just witnessed and faceplants. In his tent. To be found by his son Ham. Naked. Ham leaves him there in all his glory and goes to get his brothers. Shem and Japheth were kind enough to walk backwards into the tent, averting their gaze so they could cover him, but when Dad wakes up, he is pissed. The blame game from the garden starts all over again because instead of taking responsibility for his own drunken shenanigans, he curses Ham and blesses his brothers. The punishment seems rather unfair. But alcohol isn't known for making one think clearly. And the effects can curse generations.

Noah serves as a reminder that one careless decision can destroy the reputation of even the godliest man or woman. The Bible doesn't tell us why he got drunk. Maybe he was haunted by memories of the flood and instead of choosing to bring his pain to God, he turned to the bottle. Maybe the strain of trying to rebuild a shattered world was too great for his shoulders to bear. Maybe he felt stuck in his life circumstances and drank to avoid his current reality. Attempting to avoid negative feelings is one of the primary reasons people abuse alcohol (or any mind-altering substance) today. The truth is, that it doesn't matter what the reasons were. They don't change the responsibilities of the people involved. Noah was responsible for his own actions, as was his son Ham who reacted foolishly instead of compassionately for his inebriated father. While that decision may seem insignificant on the surface, it resulted in Noah cursing Ham's family line, and the results are still affecting us all thousands of years later.

There isn't a single moment in our lives that doesn't impact our future in some way. Even the most minor decisions will directly affect our descendants and the trajectory of their life path. Nature versus nurture. Our decisions are seemingly embedded in our DNA, and we pass our constantly evolving genetics to our children. Some of these decisions are healthy, but some of them will seem like curses, such as the genetic predisposition for addiction. Exodus 34:6-7 declares, "The Lord God, compassionate and gracious, slow to anger, and abounding in lovingkindness and truth; who keeps lovingkindness for thousands, who forgives iniquity, transgression, and sin; yet He will by no means leave the guilty unpunished, visiting the iniquity of fathers on the children and on the grandchildren to the third and fourth generations." We can indeed suffer for the sins of our parents and grandparents. To get out of the "generational curse," you have to be grafted into a whole new family tree.

(Romans 11:11-36) This is only possible with the help of the Holy Spirit, who is like what Antabuse is for an alcoholic. Once we accept Him into our hearts, He makes us violently ill towards our sins and idols and breaks the chains that have kept us enslaved so we can be free in Christ.

It's a Whole New World

Being an addict is one of the greatest gifts God has given me. I realize that might be a hard pill to swallow, but it's my truth. Something that the enemy used to cause so much heartbreak has been reworked for good used to heal myself and others. I've been grafted into a new family tree. Out of God's grace, I have been saved through faith. Not because of anything I have done or because I deserved it, but because my salvation and faith are a gift from Him to be used for His greater good. (Ephesians 2:8-10)

I recently celebrated three years of sobriety from all mind-altering substances. My struggles were primarily with painkillers (after a long fight with endometriosis) and blackout alcohol binges which would make Noah look innocent in comparison. I started smoking cigarettes and drinking when I was twelve years old and was doing hard drugs by fourteen. It didn't matter what substance it was during my teenage years, and I would try it if it had any promise of numbing me from the overwhelming pain my heart felt. Depending on your upbringing, this may seem radical and rebellious. Or it may hit close to home. Each of our pasts is different, and so are the ways we cope with the hurts that we incurred from them. We all look for worldly comfort in one way or another. The truth is, it doesn't matter what you are addicted to; we are all trying to fill a God-sized hole in our hearts with something that isn't God. That's how we sometimes end up in the bar ditch on this road called life. Or rehab like I did.

John 5:1-9 has always resonated with my heart. It's about a man disabled for thirty-eight years who was lying by a pool waiting to be healed when Jesus walks up to him and asks him if he wants to get well. The man doesn't answer yes, but instead gives Jesus the reason why he thought he hadn't yet been healed. I've been there before too. But instead of Christ finding me by a therapeutic poolside location, he hit me in the head with a two-by-four in rehab (with love, of course). I was lost in the self-pity pit, wondering why life hadn't given me all of the things I felt entitled to. In my lazy self-centeredness, I had taken the easy way out, becoming a Proverbs 5:3-5 woman who had been manipulating men into financially supporting me in return for satisfying the missing desires of their lives.

I was living a double life and was entirely out of control by this point. My drinking had escalated dramatically since it was becoming harder and harder to get painkillers or kill my emotional pain. I was piling up shame and resentments faster than Pac-Man can eat dots, and I couldn't avoid the ghosts from my past anymore. My firearms had to be removed from my house after a few incidents where I threatened to end my own life (more on that in the next chapter). This predicament was even more embarrassing, considering I was a certified rifle instructor for a local 4-H shooting sports group. My slip was showing, and the harder I tried to get a handle on my ever-increasing addiction problem, the worse it got.

I found myself in a "relationship" with a married man who wouldn't leave his wife but wouldn't let me move on to live mine. He would give me money and painkillers, and in return, I was expected to be perfectly content with being his side chick. The longer this proceeded, the more I realized all of my efforts to manipulate him into leaving his wife for me weren't working. I went online and found other sugar daddies that were even richer than he was to spite him and hurt his pride. This financed lavish hunting trips and vacations, which were never enough, and invoked his extreme jealousy. I was living on autopilot and wasn't being led by the Spirit. Every day seemed like Groundhog Day: turbulent and painful in the self-created hell I was living in. My heart was hard.

On July 16th of 2018, I was riding around in the back seat of sugar daddy's pickup truck, who was entirely disgusted with my behavior at this point but still wouldn't leave me because of his own codependency and addiction issues. It was a Monday morning, and I was nursing my wounds from the previous weekend's three-day bender I went on while the boys were at their dad's. This had become my regular routine. I started the weekend at a Thirty Seconds to Mars concert with a guy I had met at a bar and ended it by waking up to find out I had blacked out again, and this time they had filmed me skinny dipping at an apartment pool making out with strangers for attention. The all too familiar disgust and the paranoia that the video footage would come out and expose who I had become was festering in my stomach by this point. I once again brought up to him the possibility of me going to rehab. We had talked about this being a good idea for at least six months, but I never once took action until that day.

Like the chess master He is, God already had all the plans in place to put me on a path towards healing. All I needed to do was take that first step and acknowledge I wanted to be well. He had all the rest taken care of. I called a friend who told me about a place her boyfriend had just gone to in Austin. Less than forty-eight hours later, on July 18th, I stumbled through the doors of rehab drunk for what will hopefully be the last time. I only realized later what a miracle that was when talking with other patients that some of them had been fighting for over six months to get in there. When God's hand is in something, obstacles will crumble with the snap of His fingers, and the path will clear right in front of you in the blink of an eye.

Before I decided to go to rehab, I called my stepdad, who now has forty-one years in recovery, to let him know I was scared and didn't want people in my small southern town to judge me. His response was "Honey, people are already judging you. Give them something good to judge you for". So, I did. I got professional help. Not everyone needs that level of intervention to stop drinking or using. There are many different paths to freedom. This was just my path.

Check, Checkmate

My time in rehab was an eye-opening experience. I was in detox for seven days while they weaned me off of the painkillers, then transitioned to rehab within the same building for the remaining thirty. I did not go to a cush luxury location like Hazelden or Betty Ford. I went to a ghetto rehab in Austin. Had I gone to a high-end place, I'm not sure I would have taken the experience as serious long term. I was caught up in the delusion that the world owed me a fantastic existence at that point in my life. God needed to bring me back to the basics and strip my spirit of entitlement. I was in desperate need of a lesson in humility. The wine I was drinking was killing me, made with the sour grapes of resentments I was carrying. I had to be crushed to become new wine. Rehab was the beginning of a crushing life season because my old self needed to die before it killed me.

I was very naive about spiritual warfare at this point, but I can liken my time in rehab to watching a cosmic chess game play out between God and satan within those walls. Even though I grew up in the church, I was blinded to the possibility of this because I didn't take the Word literally yet. Any talk about demons was entirely outside my comfort zone. If that's where you find yourself right now reading this, I understand your reservations. Please try to postpone judgment and hang in there.

It seemed that for every chess piece that satan moved, God was there to counter it. For example, within twenty-four hours after I was admitted into detox, a girl I will call Kay checked into the facility that I now suspect was suffering from demonic possession. I don't make that claim lightly, and I would have thought you were crazy three years ago if you had told me that. But I've seen things in this sobriety journey that I can't unsee, and I now fully believe that demonic possession is possible. Jesus clearly thought this was possible, as he spent plenty of time casting out demons during His short stay on earth. It was unsettling watching Kay's severe emotional outbursts, random convulsions, and sexually manipulative tendencies. Most of the time, I was waiting for her head to spin around and the split pea soup to make an appearance. God already knew the enemy had planned this, so He had already placed a woman named Felicia in detox with me. She became my amazing sister in Christ, whom I have remained friends with even to this day. Felicia taught me a lot about the unseen spiritual battle taking place all around us. She pointed me to the armor of God, fasting, and prayer so that I wouldn't be fighting this battle defenseless.

The last night Kay was there was one of the longest nights of my life. She was transitioning from detox to rehab, and they decided to make us roommates again.

By this time, my eyes were already opened to the fact something wasn't right within her. That night as she lay in bed, she was violently shaking back and forth. This was alternated between her sitting up and growling, pulling her hair, and hitting the things around her. I was frozen in fear, but something inside of me told me that I just needed to start praying for her. So, I did. Quietly to myself praying she wouldn't hear me. The more I prayed, the worse Kay got. She started sneezing violently, and her behavior escalated. I prayed harder. Then all of a sudden, she stopped around 4 am. I just lay there quietly, and about 5 am I finally drifted off to sleep out of sheer exhaustion. When I woke up at 6 am she was gone. She was in the process of checking herself out of rehab, and I never saw her again.

The enemy's next move was to use a sexually inappropriate male counselor who only wanted to talk about my past experiences for his own sick pleasure. God conquered the enemy's pawn by moving in a queen. After an incident where the male counselor laughed off a situation during group meditation where an older man with wet brain started making comments about masturbating to the sight of me laying there, I was switched to a fantastic female counselor named LB. I would have given up on that place (and probably my sobriety) if it hadn't been for her. Her optimism and compassion were contagious. One of her favorite sayings was, "Don't be so hard on yourself. It's okay. We're all doing our best". I give her credit for the title of this book, and for being a light in such a dark time in my life.

The shenanigans from the enemy within those walls were endless. There were fights, people sleeping together, reality TV stars who had fallen from grace, theft, etc. One time a stripper smuggled in drugs in her snatch and was luckily removed before she could sell them to anyone. This was only discovered because after showering, she walked outside to smoke in lingerie and was almost tackled by an RA who wasn't putting up with nonsense on her watch. Then there was a suicidal homosexual man who attempted to throw himself in front of a school bus full of children because he couldn't deal with the pain of feeling like the world hated him for being who he was. Things happened so quickly within those walls that I could barely keep up. I saw people's eyes turn completely black for the first time, and I hope I never see that kind of evil gripping someone again. Rehab is ground zero for spiritual warfare.

A robber doesn't attack an empty house, and I firmly believe that everyone in there was attacked so hard in this life because the enemy didn't want them to realize their greatness. Addicts are some of the most intelligent, persistent, and clever people in the world. Our greatest weaknesses are our greatest strengths being used in a destructive pattern. I could relate to each and every person in there because we all have the same disease which is trying to kill us. There's good and evil within us all. I met some of the most gifted and talented people in the world there and saw incredible kindness in such a dark place. I saw Christ's love being shown to broken people by people who often didn't even know how much Christ loved them. The light shines brightest in the dark, and it was within those walls I truly saw the light for the first time.

Love Conquers All

We were expected to participate in the inhouse Twelve-step meetings and listen to the H&I (hospitals and institutions) speakers that came as guests. One of my first nights there, I showed up to the meeting with damp hair feeling groggy in a suboxone funk. This was the first time I met a man I will call Jacob, who was one of the H&I speakers who volunteered to speak with us about how he got sober.

I listened with the best of my patience, only catching parts of what our guests said until Jacob looked straight at me and said "If you think you are here to get sober for anyone else but yourself, you are full of shit. You can't do it for your kids, your spouse, or anyone else. You have to do it because you want it. You have to do it because you want to live. Because this disease will kill you." His words struck me like a knife to my heart. I don't remember anything else that was said, but I do remember sitting there with hot tears streaming down my face and weeping all night quietly so my roommates wouldn't hear me. Especially the one that had just gotten out of prison. I love that chick, but I wasn't about to show weakness because watching

Orange Is the New Black naturally made me an expert on prison culture. Insert sarcasm here.

About a week later, Jacob showed back up as a speaker one afternoon. He was sitting right in front of the windows, and I vaguely remembered him as a speaker from the week before. He started telling his story again, but the only thing I remember from his speech is that at the end, he started talking about God's love and went around the circle pointing to random people saying, "You are loved." He looked like he was glowing, but so did all the other sober people that would come and talk to us. I instinctively knew that I didn't have that glow at the time, but I wanted it. He looked straight at me and, with the bright light of the sun shining behind him, pointed at me and said, "YOU ARE LOVED." It felt like a lightning bolt hit me. I sat in awe and knew that was a message directly from God to me. When the meeting was over, and I got my bearings back, I went over to him and thanked him. He told me he would bring me a Big Book the following week and to never forget how loved I was by God.

By the time our next class was starting, the feeling of complete peace was passing, and I began to feel physically sick. I wasn't sure why the feeling of extreme nausea had come over me, but I asked for permission to go lay down for a couple of minutes. The longer I lay there, the worse I started to feel. Then I started shivering and shaking, and I couldn't stop. I can't logically explain why this happened. All I know is that no matter how hard I tried, I could not will my body into submission. When one of the RA's came to tell me to get to the next class, she realized I wasn't going to be able to. The nurse came in to check my vitals. They came to the consensus that my body was still going through a lot coming off of the painkillers and alcohol. Rest was the prescribed remedy, which was impossible. Nonetheless, I lay there for the remainder of the day and well into the night, unable to control what was going on with my body.

Looking back at it now, I wonder if someone was praying for me the way I was praying for Kay and if the convulsions were something evil leaving my body. I don't have the answers, and I won't try to explain it any further because, in the end, the explanation is not what is essential. It's how the experience impacted my journey. I deliberately choose to concentrate on learning the core message of the gospel rather than get rabbit holed and focus on what satan is doing. Loving God and loving my neighbor is more important than trying to figure out if demons have names. It's important to have a conscious awareness of the enemy's existence, but I'm not going to spend my time focusing on him anymore. Worship is what you focus on, and I'm sure as hell not worshipping that loser.

Candle in the Wind

One chapter is not enough space to cover my experiences within those thirty-seven days in Austin. I should write another book about it all before I get Alzheimer's and forget everything. Or before this disease steals another one of us who was desperately looking for the same help, I was but never found it. Unmanaged addiction is a death sentence. It is that serious. A handful of my recovery peers have already died. One of the girls was murdered by gang members in Aransas Pass. Her remains were shoved into a toolbox and later found on the side of the road. She was one of the sweetest people I have ever met and didn't deserve all of the pain she endured during her short life. We lost another girl who was a heroin addict that as a child, was sold into the sex trade and never fully recovered from the trauma she incurred. She relapsed after the birth of her child and overdosed. The loss that hurt the most was the RA that I was closest to during my stay. I later found out he had already relapsed on painkillers while I was still a resident there. He later committed suicide. Unfortunately, as this book was being edited another one of the guys was found dead in his car in a Chick-fil-A parking lot, having overdosed on heroin. If only these people knew how loved they were.

If you or someone you know is battling an addiction of any kind, please know that there is help out there. The Twelve-step recovery method has been adapted widely by fellowships of people recovering from all kinds of addictions, compulsive behaviors, and mental addictions. Fellowships now have groups in various categories, which include: alcohol, various drug addictions, cluttering, codependency, debt, eating disorders, gambling, love, obsessive skin pickers, racism, sexual addiction, underearners, workaholics, etc just to name a few.[1] All addictions are serious, and there is support out there no matter what battle you might be facing.

If the Twelve-step method isn't for you, there are other alternatives: SMART Recovery, LifeRing, Women for Sobriety (WFS), SOS (Secular Organizations for Sobriety), and Moderation Management (MM) are just a few of the options out there. Find what works for you. There is also plenty of Zoom meeting options post-pandemic. I frequently go to online meeting if I need an extra meeting in addition to the weekly in-person meeting I attend. Meetings are always a reminder that I am never alone and that others share the same struggles I do. They help remove the shame the world tries to place on me and help me get outside of my head by listening and helping others. There's no living water in your head.

Live and Let Die: Killing What's Killing You

Much of the pain we suffer comes from denial. A great deal of time and energy goes into denying that there is anything wrong with us. Our pride blinds us from seeing the truth. Surrender brings dramatic relief. This is true of any struggle against things we cannot change. When we surrender and turn it over to God, the pain of resistance goes away. Even if you are mad at God, just opening the door to your heart, a little bit will allow Him to come in and work life-changing miracles.

I would be dead if I hadn't stared my addiction in the face and battled it head-on. I had to die to myself so that I could truly live. My self-centeredness, fear, resentments, and character defects were killing me. My conduit to communicate with God was blocked by these things. I couldn't hear the Holy Spirit clearly because I hadn't yet surrendered my life to Him. I held on to the illusion of control. *The Twelve and Twelve* points out that "We have seen that character defects based upon shortsighted or unworthy desires are the obstacles that block our path towards these objectives. We now clearly see that we have been making unreasonable demands upon ourselves, upon others and upon God."[2] This is still one of the biggest areas I struggle with. I still try to go down my own path, instead of walking toward Christ. When I stopped disrespecting God by debating Him on how my plans for my life are better than His plans, He was able to start working on moving the rocks out of the way in the path He wanted me to go down. He started to pull me out of the pit of darkness and back to life. I would like to spend the next chapter addressing the darkness. The beauty of light owes its existence to the dark.

ה

The Dark Night
Of The Soul

*"I will give you the treasures of darkness
and the hoards in secret places,
that you may know that it is I, the Lord
the God of Israel, who call you by your name"
-Isaiah 45:3*

"God is more glorious than the moon; He shines
brighter than the stars" *Job 25:5 NLT*[1]

That was the first verse I bookmarked in the YouVision Bible app back in October of 2016. Minutes prior to downloading the app, I had been outside staring at the moon and stars, crying out to God while I held my loaded Kimber Stainless Pro Carry II 1911 .45 ACP in my hand, ready to end it all. This wasn't the first time I had wanted to commit suicide, and it wouldn't be the last. However, it would be a life-changing moment for me, though I didn't realize its full significance at the time.

Drunk, but not my typical blackout drunk, I could feel the tall King Ranch Bluestem grass all around me as I sat in the middle of my exfather in-laws 108-acre property which held my trailer where my boys and I lived. Life looked nothing like I had planned. I was divorced, depressed, and had no family of my own in Texas. I couldn't understand for the life of me how I had ended up where I was. I begged God to stop my heart right then so that my body wouldn't have to be found with my brains blown all over the grass that I was surrounded by. He didn't listen. That was my main complaint with Him. It seemed like He was never listening.

I cried until I didn't have any tears left anymore. I poured my heart out to Him, and in return, only heard silence as I stared through bloodshot eyes into the empty darkness. There aren't words to describe how alone and abandoned I felt at that moment. I summoned enough strength to pull the hammer back and put the gun up to my right temple when suddenly I felt the wind caress my face. It wasn't a hurricane-force wind coming to knock the gun out of my hand or anything, although that would make for a remarkable testimony. Instead, it was a gentle wind that was sufficient to catch my attention. At that moment, I heard "Don't do it until you read your Bible." It wasn't an audible voice I was hearing but rather something within me. I now recognize it was the Holy Spirit, tenderly telling me what I needed to hear most in one of my darkest moments.

Years later in Biblical Hebrew class, I discovered that Ruach HaKodesh (רוח הקודש), which we translate as "Holy Spirit" can also mean breath or wind. Even saying His name encourages your lungs to take a breath when you say it. Deep breathing helps us regulate our emotions and helps to activate that part of our nervous system that takes us out of that flight or fight mode. From the very beginning in Genesis 2:7, God breathed life into Adam's nostrils, and it was then he became a living being. It is a vivid reminder of how with each breath we take, God's presence fills us with life. We are never truly alone.

When Doves Cry

I got out of that field, put my gun up, and began my mission to read the entire Bible. I started in Genesis and was terrified to finish Revelation because I hadn't found the life-changing answer I was desperately looking to find. I was still suicidal and depressed and wondered if I had heard something wrong that night. My life had only seemed to worsen throughout the year as my addictions and sexual promiscuity were spiraling out of control. Nonetheless, I pressed on and finished my first time through the Bible by the end of October in 2017.

The thought hit me that maybe I hadn't found Jesus yet because I hadn't had a water submersion baptism. To this day, I have a tough time accepting God's grace and always tend to look for a works-based solution to earn His love. Spoiler alert: that's never the answer. His grace is a gift, and He chooses us first. On November 5th, 2017, I made the public declaration to accept Jesus into my heart and got dunked in the water trough at the Cowboy Church I attended at that time. I came out of the water disappointed and confused because I didn't see the Holy Spirit descend from heaven like a dove as Jesus did after He was baptized (Matthew 3:16, Mark 1:10, Luke 3:22, John 1:32). If I ever had a public ministry, I always wanted to name it "When Doves Cry" out of fondness for my ignorant expectation of my baptism experience. However, Prince was always very protective over his intellectual property, so I had better leave that one alone before I get sued.

My panic that something had gone wrong was only amplified when I found out after church let out that the Sutherland Springs Church shooting had taken place only forty-five minutes down the road while I was being baptized. The attack was the deadliest mass shooting in Texas history, killing twenty-five and wounding twenty-two others before the shooter committed suicide. I knew logically that it wasn't my fault, but somehow in my sick mind, I thought that the two events were somehow correlated and that this was God's way of telling me I was evil. Satan is such a dick.

4 X 4 Aim for Kindness

Even through the darkness I was experiencing, I kept plugging away at trying to find my life purpose and trying to find a God who seemed elusive and absent. In the spring of 2018, I was sitting in church when I noticed Kevin and Audrey McCleary sitting in front of me. The couple's only two children, Madison and Tanner, had been killed in a car accident on the way to school a year prior on January 18th, 2017. I had briefly met them before when Tanner had shown interest in the shooting sports rifle program I was coaching at the time. He was an avid hunter and outdoorsman and had the best sense of humor. I was amazed by his boldness when he told me at rifle orientation that shotguns were better than rifles. He had his father's charming coy smile and his beautiful mother's kind heart. I found out after he went to heaven that we were birthday buddies, and it brings a smile to my face every June 8th when I think of him celebrating with Jesus every year on our birthday. I never had the privilege of meeting Madi, but she was a champion weightlifter and had the same stunning smile and bold spirit her brother did. It didn't seem fair that God would allow their seemingly bright futures to be snuffed out before they had fully lived their lives on this planet. Through the #spreadkindnessformandt movement, their legacy lives on one act of kindness at a time as others post photographs of the kind acts they are doing throughout the world in remembrance of these two incredible lives taken too soon.

Sitting behind them in the church that day, I was in awe that they could still worship after they had their whole world ripped from them. At that moment, an idea came to me. For years I had thrown a skeet shoot for my birthday party, but this year with my depression and life spiraling out of control, it didn't seem like my birthday was a reason to celebrate. A tiny voice from within told me to go up to Audrey and ask her if we could throw a charity skeet shoot in memory of Tanner for his birthday. Something within me summoned courage, and I went up to her after church and asked her if she was open to that possibility. That was the spark for the 4 X 4 Aim for Kindness event.

Audrey and I had lunch one afternoon shortly after that day, where she told me that she had the vision for a four-competition shooting event: rifle, shotgun, and women/men pistol. It was during that lunch, while staring into her face, that I realized the depths of how genuinely selfish it was that I wanted to end my own life. Her son would have no more earthly birthdays, and here I was, wanting to put an end to mine by my hand. This event saved my life in more ways than one, and we raised over $13K donating $3,300 to four local charities in honor of Tanner's thirteenth birthday. I'm still slightly jealous he got to spend the day with Jesus, but I know it's not my time yet. I have to trust that God still has me here for His reasons and focus more on Him rather than my pain.

Page of Pentacles

The Father's Day after the shoot, my friend Cynthia and I took our annual single mom's Father's Day trip together while our boys were at their dads. We decided to go to New Orleans and Slidell, Louisiana, to fish for red drum. She is the avid fisher of the two of us, but I still managed to catch a bigger fish than she did, even with a radial head fracture that I acquired from falling on our Segway tour the day before. I refused to go to the hospital until we went home and proceeded to drink my way through the pain. I'm surprised I came home from that trip because she threatened to feed me to the fishes for numerous reasons. My fish, having been bigger, was the least obnoxious one.

Being back in New Orleans, we naturally had to get some beignet donuts at Cafe Du Monde. Being the alcoholic attention seeker I am, we also had to make our pilgrimage to Bourbon Street so I could earn a neck full of beads. Cynthia was given one white set of beads dubbed her "purity beads" that she liked to point out that she did not earn, in stark contrast to my overflowing neck full of fleshly trophies. However, we couldn't leave the city until I had another tarot card reading.

If you remember from chapter three, I had a tarot card reading in NOLA at the age of fourteen when my mom took us on a road trip there because she was craving those famous beignets. Since I was already divorced by thirty-five with four children (I had two stepdaughters in addition to our two sons), I needed to know the rest of the story. On our last day there, I hunted down a tarot card reader in Jackson Square. She told me that I would find the love of my life in six weeks, that I would be financially stable in ten months, and I would live a life filled with happiness. Remember what she said because I will come back to this in the next chapter on love.

Upon returning home, I posted some of my NOLA trip on Facebook (let's be honest, the world didn't need to see all of the pictures). That was when a group of my Catholic friends reached out and said I needed to meet with them immediately. I went over to their house, and they asked me if I knew how serious it was that I was playing with tarot cards. I was too scared to mention the ones under my bed at this point, so I told them that I did not. They asked me to sit with them and write down a list of all of the things I could think of that I had done wrong. I might have left out my deepest darkest secrets, but I gave them a list that would make any nun blush. They went through the list and made me repent of all of my wrongdoings. It was at that point that they laid hands on me and started praying in what I now know to be tongues. This scared the crap out of me because I had no idea what was going on, and my body started feeling hot. Immediately after leaving there, I took a handful of painkillers, smoked a cigarette, and tried to chase the incident out of my mind.

Matthew 12:43-45 tells us that "When the unclean spirit has gone out of a person, it passes through waterless places seeking rest, but finds none. Then it says: 'I will return to my house from which I came.' And when it comes, it finds the house empty, swept, and put in order. Then it goes and brings with it seven other spirits eviler than itself, and they enter and dwell there, and the last state of that person is worse than the first." I have seen the accuracy of this verse first hand. When good-meaning Christians cast out demons, but the person hasn't asked the Holy Spirit to enter their heart, they are left with an empty house just asking for more trouble. The time between when I was baptized until the time that I checked into rehab was the craziest time of my life, especially after the tongues incident. When evil is cast out, the Holy Spirit has to be asked in. If not, the evil will return sevenfold.

Nick at Night

My experience coming out of rehab is analogous with an infant coming out of her mother's womb. I was reborn in many ways. John 3:1-15 talks about the experience of being born again. A man named Nicodemus came to Jesus in the dark, which is literal and symbolic darkness since he hadn't had a spiritual awakening yet. Jesus told him that unless he was born again that he could not see the kingdom of God. Nicodemus asked Him how this was possible, to which Jesus answered "Truly, truly, I say to you, unless one is born of water and the Spirit, he cannot enter the kingdom of God. That which is born of the flesh is flesh, and that which is born of the Spirit is spirit." The last mention of Nicodemus in scripture is when he brings myrrh and aloe to anoint Jesus' body for burial. Not only did he bring the ointment, but he also brought seventy-five pounds worth, which is a significant indicator Jesus had touched him in a heartfelt way. He was risking possible public humiliation and shame to honor the Savior with such boldness.

It's a profound experience being truly reborn. Although I was baptized with water on November 5th,

I accredit that day in rehab where Jacob pointed to me in the circle and declared "You are loved," as the day I started to let the Spirit into my heart so that I could be reborn. I did not have a personal relationship with Jesus at that point but hearing those words set something on fire in my soul that set me on a path of chasing Him with my entire being. We are all three-part beings like the Trinity (who is Father, Son, and Holy Spirit). We are body (flesh), soul (mind, thoughts, and heart), and spirit (our innermost self).

Additionally, it's important to note we are attacked by three enemies: the world, the devil, and the flesh. God tends to work on us from the inside out. First, He typically works on our spirit, which in turn rewires our mind, affecting the choices we make with our bodies to make us more Christlike. Satan, on the other hand, tends to attack us from the outside in. If our flesh can be tempted to follow the world with our bodies by chasing false promises of comfort, then our souls and our minds drift farther away from unity with our creator and true peace. Satan has been using these tactics for centuries.

It's Always Darkest Before the Dawn

I am fascinated with the story of St. John of the Cross.[2] He was a tiny little Carmelite friar who was a major figure of the Counter-Reformation in Spain during the Spanish Inquisition. He is most closely identified with the phrase "the dark night of the soul," even though in his work The Dark Night, he never uses the term.

Born into extreme poverty, he lived a tough life by all standards. He was incarcerated in a monastery, locked in a ten-by-sixteen-foot cell, and endured persecution/public lashings. Like Christ, he was tortured by the religious people of his time. Throughout it all, he poured himself into his poetry and worked reforming the Carmelite Order with St. Teresa of Avila.

St. John saw these periods of darkness and suffering as opportunities by God to lean more into Him. We tend to think of darkness as something evil. However, the original word he used for dark in Spanish was "la noche oscura," translated as the "obscure night." St. John understood these as times where what God was doing is obscure/mysterious, where it is hard to know where He is and what He is doing. When the comforts of life were stripped away, and the only thing left to rely on was Christ, God could then come in like a surgeon and remove the sick parts of the heart that are separated from Him. He says in one of his poems:[3]

> *"My soul is detached*
> *From every thing created,*
> *And raised above itself*
> *Into a life delicious,*
> *Of God alone supported.*
> *And therefore I will say,*
> *That what I most esteem*
> *Is that my soul is now*
> *Without support, and with support"*

Sooner or later, all of us who choose to surrender our lives to Christ will have to be separated from that which is earthly, whether that be this side of heaven or the next. The dark night of the soul, though a painful process, gives us freedom from the chains that ensnare us so that we can be free to walk humbly with God in our purpose. The pain in these dark seasons helps us shed our paradigms and the things we allow to construct our life's meaning. They strip us from finding our identities in ourselves, relationships with others, habits, or belief systems. It falls back to our basic instinct to want dominion over our lives and our destinies, and God needs to break us of our self-reliance so we find our identity in Him. During this significant and challenging transition, we are allowed to die to ourselves so that we can be reborn.

As we have previously discussed, our perceived identities are formed as a product of the interconnectedness we have with all of humanity. They are manifested in our daily actions as a result of how we integrate our experiences with others. This isn't where our true identity should be found as a born-again Christian. (Galatians 2:20) Our identity should be found in our Father. The dark night of the soul is an ejection from autopilot that allows us to reconnect with who we really are when His Truth doesn't line up with our truth. It can be brought on by any number of factors ranging from life-changing tragedy to illness or depression. Sometimes the reason for onset is more subtle, such as having an epiphany that you don't know what your purpose on this planet is. Everything can suddenly seem meaningless. Feelings of intense sadness, frustration, and hopelessness are common descriptions of this spiritual crisis. The most painful part for me was that it felt like God removed His presence, and I couldn't hear His voice.

In February of 2021, Texas went through what we refer to as SnowVid 2021. Almost a full year into the COVID pandemic, we got hit with much higher snow levels than we are used to in a state that, for the most part, doesn't snow. Our electrical grids were not prepared for this, and many of us went without power or water for days in houses that were not built for cold weather. I work in the hospice field and was already burnt out after seeing the physical and emotional turmoil all around me daily throughout the year prior. I'm also prone to experiencing seasonal affective depression, so by the time this literal storm blew in, it was already the recipe for the perfect storm in my heart. I once again found myself in a dark night of the soul season. My journal entry for February 16th, 2021 was:

"Being without power or water the past forty-eight hours has brought to my attention how fixated I am on my external surroundings for happiness. I've been mad at you, and depressed. I'm putting my hope in the wrong things. You are all I really need. I'm grumbly and miserable to be around. I've been listening to my own negative inner voice more than I have your Spirit. I want more than anything to feel your presence. I miss you and I know it's not you that has strayed far away. I'm sorry and I love you."

I want to say that I snapped out of it instantly after praying that prayer. Unfortunately, looking back through my journal, it was about three weeks before I saw the light again. Even though I had been reborn for two years by this point, I was still hit hard with a life-stealing depression that left me paralyzed and barely able to get out of bed for days. This is why it is so important to journal. Because during this painful time, I could look back to what I had previously written about all of the ways He has already been faithful in my life and the prior instances He had delivered me. I still get hit with depression/suicidal ideation, and will possibly even experience another dark night of the soul episode. But at least I can call the enemy out on his lies when he tells me I won't survive. We are all inclined to forget His faithfulness, so journaling can remind us of what we tend to forget when we are in the pit.

If you are going through an episode similar to this, know that you aren't alone in your struggles. Many mature Christians undergo dark night of the soul episodes. Mother Teresa felt the silence of God for most of her life, as was discovered in her private writings after her death. Martin Luther experienced multiple intense episodes throughout his lifetime, typically brought on by illness or tragedy. C.S. Lewis was open about his struggles with dark night episodes after the loss of his wife Joy. Yet the sentiment of this dark season of life is best sung by Andrew Peterson in his song *The Silence of God*:[4]

"It's enough to drive a man crazy;
it'll break a man's faith
It's enough to make him wonder if he's ever been sane
When he's bleating for comfort
from Thy staff and Thy rod
And the heaven's only answer is the silence of God"

If you remember back in school, the teacher was always silent during the exam. I've noticed a pattern in my life looking back that if God was silent, then I need to pay attention to what I should be learning. This isn't always the case. Sometimes these things happen and I won't find out the reason during my lifetime. No matter what, the answer has always been that He uses these intense seasons as a way to bring me closer to Him if I let Him. When we can't see His hand, we must trust His heart.

Part Sinner, Part Saint, Part Sufferer

Have you ever struggled through a season where you couldn't hear God? Is it possible He is communicating with you in a different way than you are used to so as to break you from depending on a pattern of communication instead of a relationship with Him? God spoke in many ways throughout scripture. Sometimes He came in a burning bush, and other times He spoke in a gentle wind. Many times, He used other people to relay His message. Just as a parent doesn't talk to their adult child in the same ways they did when they were an infant, God will change how He speaks to you as you grow in your walk with Him.

Ask Him if this is the case. He gives wisdom generously to all without finding fault to all who ask. (James 1:15)

Do you feel like every day is a wrestling match just to function? Let's say you already have asked God why you aren't hearing Him, and all you hear back is the sound of your own blood pressure rising. Continue to wrestle with Him. Wrestling is an intimate activity where two people have to be close. Jacob wrestled with God back in Genesis and came out blessed as Israel in the end. Maybe the case is that you are wrestling with unrepentant sin and unforgiveness like I was? I couldn't hear from God clearly until I admitted I had a problem and needed to get rid of all the rocks of sin blocking my conduit to Him. God is perfect and Holy, and sin separates us from Him. Once I acknowledged that my sin and unforgiveness were the problem and surrendered those problems to Him, the flood gates were open and I entered a season where I heard from Him in overwhelming ways. My life still needed much pruning after rehab, but at least I was connected to the Vine again.

Maybe you have already done all these things, and you are living a reasonably sin-free life like Mother Teresa. Not many people are on that level, but just for argument's sake let's say you can't think of one area in your life where you need to repent or forgive someone, but you have still found yourself in the dark night of the soul. If it's any small consolation, remember that Christ Himself felt the sting of God's silence at the end of His life also. Mark 15:34 tells us some of His last words on the cross were: "Eloi, Eloi, lema sabachthani?" (Which means "My God, My God, why have you forsaken me?)[5] We can see in hindsight that God had not forsaken Him but that He had a greater plan in mind. Our ways are not His ways. (Isaiah 55:8-9) He can use pain to bring a saint closer to Him and help another suffering, just as He did with Christ. Those who are called to Christ are all part sinner, part saint, and part sufferer. Sometimes we won't have the answers we seek on this side of heaven. Don't lose faith and know that He is working all things for good in those who love Him. (Romans 8:28) Your pain will not be wasted.

Have you ever been so chronically depressed that you wanted to die? Never forget, the dark always appears darkest before dawn. There is always help out there. Never give up. Pain is your body's megaphone shouting that something is wrong. Being depressed doesn't mean you are weak. It means you have been abiding in your own strength for too long. Lean into Him and reach out to others. The enemy wants you to feel alone and isolated, so he can continue to whisper lies into your soul. I have "Who told you that...?" which is part of Genesis 3:11 tattooed on my foot. Originally it was God asking who told Adam and Eve that they were naked in the garden (it was the snake, by the way), but the verse can apply to any voice that isn't coming from God. Who told you that you are worthless? Who told you that you were stupid? Who told you that you were ugly? Who told you that your life isn't worth living? All of those thoughts cross my mind on a routine basis, and I have to remember that they aren't the voice of God.

Who told you help isn't available? If you are struggling with thoughts of suicide this very moment, know that there is a National Suicide Prevention Lifeline that is available twenty-four hours a day. The number is 1-800-273-8255 in the US, and the website is https://suicidepreventionlifeline.org.[6] Who told you that counseling is for losers? Many of the world's most successful people seek professional help to learn where their defective thought patterns could be improved for optimal health and wellness. There is no shame in seeing a counselor. The sooner we break the stigma of mental health problems and start talking about these things in the open, the less we will be attacked. Who told you that no one cares? You aren't alone. Please reach out to someone today if you are experiencing a dark night of the soul season. My sincerest prayer for you today is that no matter what life throws at you, you know that God is always with you and that you are never alone. YOU are loved.

ו

Love And Dating: The Ultimate Quest for Boaz

Love isn't complicated,
people are.
-Author Unknown

The inner me is a Gomer. Who is Gomer, you might ask? She was the idolatrous wife of the prophet Hosea who was the last prophet God raised up in Israel to try to get the people to repent before the exile to Assyria. The first three chapters of his book discuss the sordid details of their stormy marriage. God directed him to marry a harlot and allowed all of this to take place as a lesson to Israel, who had been just as faithless to God as Gomer had been to Hosea. I thought Jonah had it bad, but Hosea's calling had to have been worse. His mission was to wait for his hoe to become a housewife, all in the eye of the public.

Why on earth would I be crazy enough to compare myself to a harlot in a book that my mama and Lord only knows who else will read? I thought you would never ask. Because I've lost my mind. Slightly kidding. But If I am to give you an accurate representation of my life story, I can't leave out the ugly parts. That includes the parts that I would like to keep secret. I can't hide in the baggage either. The enemy still tries to throw my past back at me, to keep me stuck in the shame pit of self-condemnation. The more I loathe myself and hide my history, the less I can help others who still struggle in the same areas. I'm stripping him of that power and reminding my inner Gomer that she has been forgiven and that God has lovingly guided her home. The devil can shove it. In the famous words of Pamela Pumpkin, "Squash satan and kick him in the crotch."[1]

As previously discussed, I have never felt secure in this world. Self-admittedly, at times I'm a little neurotic in my quest for comfort and predictability. After I was raped, it sent me down an ugly spiral where I attempted to chase worldly security in relationships, only to find that it was fleeting and unobtainable. Ira Israel talks about the myth of romance in Western civilization as something that modern lovers do to find the missing part of themselves. He points out our tendency to view ourselves as "inherently unwhole" and seek to find our "missing piece" in the form of a soulmate.[2] True love and protection will never be found in another human being. It only comes from above. Looking for it anywhere else amounts to the idolatry of the heart.

The Lord tells Hosea to declare to his brothers and sisters of Israel:

"For she said, 'I will go after my lovers, who give me my bread and my water, my wool and my flax, my oil and my drink. Therefore I will hedge up her way with thorns, and I will build a wall against her, so that she cannot find her paths. She shall pursue her lovers, but she will not overtake them, and she shall seek them but shall not find them. Then she will say, 'I will go and return to my first husband, for it was better for me than now.' And she did not know that it was I who gave her the grain, the wine, and the oil, and who lavished on her silver and gold, which they used for Baal." (Hosea 2:5-8)

This is precisely what I have done in my romantic pursuits throughout life. Similar to Gomer and the nation of Israel, I chased *my* impure plans with selfish ambition and repeatedly broke his heart by seeking other lovers instead of putting God first. Like the song says, I was "looking for love in all the wrong places". Therefore, He allowed my path to be hedged with thorns. This way, I would repent, remove the thorns, and start looking towards Him and His will for my life. Through these pruning seasons, I've learned that true satisfaction only comes from the Lord. I can see in hindsight that He allowed all of the pain so that I would come back home to Him, just as Gomer did to Hosea.

For simplicity's sake, I will focus the rest of this chapter on dating after my divorce and during my sobriety. I could write a whole separate book on what went wrong with my marriage, and maybe one day I will. However, the stories from the last three years are way more entertaining, and I remember them with more mental clarity. I have learned so many hilarious and heartbreaking lessons through my trials and tribulations in this specific area. So much so, that when it was recommended that I write a book in one of the areas I struggle in most, my nine-year-old son (whom I didn't think was listening) immediately suggested that I write a book on dating. That kid is pretty dang perceptive. The areas make us want to strangle our children at times that will make them successful adults one day if continually channeled in a positive direction. Proud mommy moment, even if it was embarrassing at the time.

Wrestling With God: Two Peas in a Pod

While in rehab, I finally concluded that it wasn't wise or healthy to date a married man. This should have been a no-brainer on an ethical level, but I was pretty screwed up in the head back then. My heart was hard. It still hurts to know that I was capable of doing the things that I did and that I could act so callously without remorse. However, there is a reason the rearview mirror on a vehicle is smaller than the windshield. Changing the past is impossible, and I can only try to do better in the future from here on out.

Nevertheless, getting rid of the sugar daddy didn't ditch my undiscovered deep-rooted codependency issues. So, when Jacob (the one from chapter four) came into the picture, I walked right into that thirteenth stepper's trap like a kid climbing into a white van looking for candy. You might be wondering, "What is a thirteenth stepper?" Not officially part of any twelve-step recovery program, the "thirteenth step of recovery" is when a more experienced member of a twelve-step group- a man or a woman- pursues a romantic relationship with a new group member. It is discouraged to start any new relationships within the first year of sobriety because someone in the beginning stages of recovery is incredibly vulnerable. Often still in a fog, they cannot think as clearly or rationally as they will after time passes because their brains still need time to rewire themselves and repair the damage done. There is a power play here where the newcomer is at risk for being taken advantage of, as well as derailing their newfound recovery efforts. With only three years of sobriety, I can typically tell when a newbie walks into a meeting as if they were wearing a neon banner over their heads. They don't have the same glow that a person with a more extended period of sobriety has. There is a night and day difference to a person's appearance and mannerisms.

I genuinely thought I would find the love of my life that week because of the tarot card reading I had in New Orleans six weeks earlier. The enemy will use whatever he can to try to derail your future, including your ignorance/ superstitious nature, as he did with me in this scenario. Against the guidance of my counselor LB, (and my more experienced peers in the program) I started to date Jacob.

My friend Johnna teases me by comparing me to a girl in a TikTok video who says "Red flags? My favorite color is red!" As much as it makes me want to stab her, admittedly, I love her for it because it is true. My codependent self loves to overlook glaring red flags, and that was indeed the case with Jacob. He spoiled me, treating me like a princess. He went above and beyond to take over everything, letting me relax and find my bearings. He taught me a lot about Christ and the Bible. He introduced me to the movie Ragamuffin by David Leo Schultz[3], which forever changed my life and led me to a new group of amazing friends all over the country. Shout out TB! Desperate to be loved and have some level of normalcy in my chaotic life, I let Jacob have the reigns. It all seemed too good to be true. That first week was a magical time. He is a semi-famous musician, having recorded two records in Nashville. I would watch him play at shows, and he would serenade me in private. It was all very romantic. So, when he got the opportunity to perform in Pennsylvania, I agreed to go with him in a New York minute so I could see the Big Apple for the first time after his show.

Before we even left, things slowly started to change, as they frequently do in a toxic relationship with two broken people. Everything started to turn into an argument when things weren't how he wanted. He demanded to go through my wardrobe and get rid of anything that he didn't think was modest enough to wear in public. He went through my phone and deleted any photos or contacts that weren't female or direct family. Then he took control of my finances. To be perfectly honest, I still was horrible at adulting at this point, so my lack of wanting to take responsibility for my own life opened myself up to being taken advantage of. So, when the attorney general's office finally released the money that was relinquished from my back child support, Jacob was right there to offer to manage it for me. Except I never saw it again. He took $2,000 and told me I owed him for the New York trip, even though the original arrangement was that the trip was a gift from him.

We started to fight more, and the fights became more serious. Dad wasn't allowed to visit for his annual Christmas trip. This should have been a huge red flag, but we had already made our relationship public. In my mind, I thought I had already done enough damage to my reputation by this point, and leaving him would symbolize failure once again. I was isolated from almost all of my former friends, either by him or from shame. One day I got a Facebook message from an older woman demanding that Jacob pay her the money back that she had given him. Apparently, during the time period I was in rehab he led her to believe they were dating and she was helping him financially. He dumped her for me once I came along, and she was justifiably pissed. He tried sweet-talking his way out of it, but the seeds of doubt in my mind had already grown into an ugly plant by this point. The final straw was when my son's ADHD medication started going missing. I confronted him about it, and he pushed me. I pushed him back, and when he realized I wasn't going down without a fight he apologized immediately.

That incident was the straw that broke the camel's back. When he declined to take a home drug test, I broke things off. It wasn't pleasant. Was I innocent in all of this? No. Far from it. I was emotional and acted immature a great deal of the time throughout the relationship. I don't hold any bitterness in my heart for what happened, and I hope he forgives me for all of the ways I hurt him. The point in bringing any of this up isn't to slander him, it is to solidify the notion that two people in the early stages of recovery, like we both were, should not be dating 99% of the time. They both need time to remove the idols from their heart, clear their heads, and let God fix the wounds from the past before they are healthy enough to be in a relationship again. I was replacing one addiction for another by dating Jacob and bringing my baggage with me.

What's Love Got to Do with It?

Aristotle, one of the world's most renowned thinkers, was quoted as saying "It is of the nature of desire not to be satisfied, and most men live only for the gratification of it."[4] This is seen over and over again in the majority of our culture's art, films, and songs which show lovers overcoming insurmountable obstacles to be together. We love the chase, and we confuse passion with love. We have created a fairy tale illusion in our culture that without passion there can be no intimacy. Lust is confused with love. De Rougemont believed that in passion we subconsciously seek suffering, which is not conducive to functional romantic relationships.[5] The root word for passion is *patior*, which means to suffer. Just think on that next time you hear "the passion of the Christ". One of my complaints with English is that our words don't express their profound meanings in the same way the original Hebrew, Greek, or Latin do. This is what inspired me to learn Biblical Hebrew to have a deeper understanding of God's love letter to us.

We tend to throw the "L" word around loosely, using the same word for how we feel about pumpkin spice lattes as we do about our children. The ancient Greeks had many different words for love, but the four found in scripture are storge, philia, eros, and agape.[6] Storge love is the natural, familial love found within a household. An example of this type of love would be the love shown by a parent for a child. Phila is the type of love that we refer to as "brotherly love" and is where the city of Philadelphia got its name. Christ called us in John 13:35 to love our brothers and sisters in Christ with this kind of love if we are to be faithful followers of His.

Eros is the Greek word for sensual or romantic love. We tend to confuse it with erotic love, which is the type that is mainly portrayed in Hollywood. When perverted, eros seeks its own interest and satisfaction. It wants to possess the object of love. This is the type of love that Jacob and I had. Passionate and fierce, it went up in flames quickly like a fire that is too hot because it started off with too much diesel accelerant. True love is agape love, which describes the immeasurable love from God. It is perfect, unconditional, sacrificial, and pure. The Holy Spirit is the only one who can bring true agape love, as seen in John 21:15-17 when Jesus is asking John if he loves him. Jesus asks him "Do you *agape* me?", and Peter who hasn't received the Holy Spirit at Pentecost yet, answers that he *phileos* him. You don't know what you don't know.

After dating Jacob, I took a season of healing and went to a Christian therapist and worked on myself. I spent those eight months growing in my walk with Christ, and He worked on healing my heart in many ways. In December of 2019, I started talking with a man from church. We had met in a church singles group two years prior, but I was still drinking heavily back then and was a hot mess so it wasn't good timing. He was a sweet man who came from a fantastic family. Two years later, we started dating. He was also a believer, but he didn't have the same passion I did for Christ. He was perfectly content with just going to church on Sundays and going through the motions the rest of the week. No judgment here for that, but being in recovery, my entire life is centered around staying plugged into my higher power. If I'm not swimming forward, then I'm drifting back. My survival depends on my faith *with* works because I'm not a "normie" (someone who can drink or use drugs without the obsessive need leading to addiction). My addictions will always try to lure me towards death.

Being the stubborn woman that I am, I was trying to be the leader in the relationship. What can I say? I grew up with the Spice Girls "girl power" mentality as a 90's kid. I have control issues, and due to my hard-headed nature, I need a strong-willed man of God that is very rooted in Christ. I wasn't capable of giving him agape love because I was trying to conform him to my expectations of what a Godly husband should look like instead of loving him how he was. You should never date someone based on their potential. Date them for who they actually are. My therapist pointed out that the longer I continued to date him, the more unloving I was acting towards him because I was blocking him from finding the right person God designed for him. It hurt, but I wanted God's best for both of us, so I broke things off. We tried to date again a few months later, but it was more of the same, so I ended things for the last time. He is a great person, and we are still friendly when we see each other in town. I pray that he finds his person, and they live a life full of passion for Christ in the way God designed them.

Through our relationship, I learned it is vital for both parties to know who their master is (Christ) to be biblically yoked. Once I was a slave to my addictions and the flesh, and now I am a slave to Christ. (Galatians 4:7) Once you are solidified in the freedom of your slave status (I recognize that is confusing), then you are free to seek your mission for God's kingdom. God doesn't need you to do anything for Him, but He does desire to see you using the gifts/talents He designed you with to draw others to Him so they can also have a personal relationship with him. If you are suffering through a long season of singleness, maybe God wants to work with you to find your mission before you find your mate? If this is you, pray about it. Then pray some more. Shoot even if this isn't you, pray for someone. The world can always use more prayers.

T + G/42 = Lord Only Knows

It blows my mind that as someone who disliked algebra so much, I tend to live my life trying to solve my life by the same logical methodology. My natural inclination is to assume that if there's T (me) plus G/42 (God over the 42 different ways I'm going to try to manipulate the situation to my advantage), then it should all balance out to *my* desired outcome on the other side of that equal sign. I knew I should have paid more attention in class on how to find solutions because I cannot figure out the equation on how to date in the twenty-first century. Still struggling with math as well, so please show me some grace if my subpar math metaphors are making you cringe. We're all doing our best.

Technology and social norms have changed the way people date in today's modern landscape. It's incredibly frustrating for someone who likes systems in place. I think I'm finding the solution to an Algebra equation, and the subsequent potential date shows up working on Geometry. At least Mr. Geometry is participating in math class because he could be like the online date I had this summer who had completely checked out of class high on LSD. True story. I didn't even know people did LSD outside of Burning Man anymore, but I've been out of the game for a while. It's hip to be square.

My friend Laura bought me some relief from online dating mint placebos for Christmas this past year. I'm seriously considering taking them because I heard if you believe in a placebo hard enough it will work. Being superstitious and religious is tricky because it occasionally makes it hard to discern whether God's hand is at work or if I'm wandering into new terrain loaded with land mines. Online dating, in particular, has made for a variety of entertaining disappointments. Date after date, I come to terms with God's sovereignty and become more accepting that the world is a strange place.

For example, I met a guy online with the last name "Priest", so I thought surely God was delivering Mr. Right this time. Tasha Priest. That name was absolutely screaming for a more prominent ministry calling. He even volunteered to come over on our second date with a chainsaw to cut a tree off my roof. I mean, who doesn't want a second date with a random stranger and a chainsaw? I saw no danger in that whatsoever. It all seemed divinely ordained. I mean, why else would the tree have fallen on my house? All looked promising until a couple of weeks later, when a group of us went tubing down the river, and the Priest acted like a frat boy on steroids. Luckily, I had Laura with me on that one and she needed to get home which got me out of that one. Buddy system for the win.

Then there was the Leprechaun entrepreneur who casually monopolized the conversation by talking about his recent breakup, his failing start-up company, and how he was looking for a patient girl to help him while he got back on his feet. Ten points for brutal honesty, negative ten points for his ability to market himself as a catch for a sum total of zero chance for a second date. Nice guy, no judgment, but why is there this incessant need in our culture that we need to find our soulmate to fix all of our life's problems? If you are drowning, you have to learn how to swim before you can synchronize swim with someone else. Being single again, he was in the perfect position to recover from his past hurts and create a life that made him happy. Instead, he was back on the dating scene with a gaping gunshot wound to the chest looking for someone to come along with a small band aid and make it all better. It's easier to see happiness as dependent on external circumstances than it is to do the work finding it within. I'm no different than he is though, so when I say no judgment, I truly mean it. Our interaction was like looking in a mirror (more on mirrors in a later chapter). This long season of singleness continues to allow me to work with God on changing my heart so I can be healthier when the right person comes along. Happy healthy people attract happy healthy people.

This brings me to the Serbian. Raise your hand if you had to Google where Serbia is because you didn't know it off the top of your head. Yeah, same here. No shame friend. I was really attracted to the Serbian. He also likes to swim in the deep end of the thought pool. I love that he had no problems calling me out on my crap. On our first date, he looked straight in the eyes and said "I'm going to need you to stop being so hard on yourself because that's a huge red flag you are going to be too hard on me too." Ouch. Although it pains me to admit, I do like a dominant man who calls it like it is. We would meet at a hookah bar and play chess until two in the morning, engaging in deep, meaningful conversations. As the months passed on, his own red flags started to appear. Like the fact I couldn't ever go to his house. He said it was because of his European mother living there with him and that he doesn't bring women home to the place where his daughter lives out of respect. I say that if a man doesn't respect you enough to start incorporating you into his life after a couple of months, then he isn't looking at you as wife material. That, my friends, is where my biggest problem was.

That scenario was never going to lead towards a healthy Biblical marriage, and as a born-again believer, I am not called to be unequally yoked. Although he identified as an Eastern Orthodox Christian, he didn't have a personal relationship with Christ. He lived more along the lines of being a practicing Buddhist. Live in the present was his motto. I speculate God used this whole scenario to snap me out of my inability to live in the present moment because I am constantly either future tripping or in the self-pity pit of the past. That character defect was blocking my ability to kick it with Christ. Still a work in progress in that area, but it's all about progress, not perfection. However, I still need to live a Kingdom-minded lifestyle while enjoying the gifts in the now. If I'm not making decisions moving towards my higher power, I am placing myself at risk of relapse. Relapse=death. Things fizzled out with the Serbian once I realized after a series of events one holiday weekend that he was never going to be able to offer me the selfless Christ-like love I was looking for and that the used car salesman in him was always going to attempt to manipulate things in his favor and farther away from Christ. I learned a lot and miss the intellectual banter, but I know God has a better plan for my life that will glorify Him.

Dating In the Twilight Zone

There is an old Yiddish proverb, "Man plans and God laughs."[7] He must currently be rolling on His sides, with tears flowing down His face and a belly ache from laughing so hard because my life is centered around planning. Surrender is not my strong suit. I'm better at wrestling with Him for control of my life. Back during the eight-month single stretch, I had started praying for a godly man. When Mr. Church Singles' group didn't work out, I realized I needed to up my prayer game. Although I don't believe God is a genie in a bottle waiting to answer prayers, I do think he wants us to bring everything to Him. He wants all of us, including our desires. Sometimes He answers them. Sometimes He doesn't. Sometimes He answers them in His own timing. I have learned that it's essential to know what you are asking for because sometimes that's precisely what you will get.

One night at a wedding a couple of years ago, I was approached by a 6'8 muscular man that looked like he could have been a Greek god while I was talking with my ex-husband and his wife. They assumed he was my date because, by all outward appearances, we looked good standing side by side, both being very tall with magnetic smiles. I laughed, explained I had never met the man, and we introduced ourselves to one another. I almost thought I was being pranked because he loved God, hunting, and from outward appearances, seemed to have it together. We sat next to one another while we ate, talked for a little while, and then he left. My heart hoped it was one of those fairy tale moments everyone talks about where when you quit looking for love, it falls right in your lap.

He Facebook friend requested me, and through our conversations, I slowly realized Mr. Right wasn't being served up on a silver platter. He was in the middle of a divorce and already had another girl pregnant (which ironically, I'm friends with now, and she's an amazing Proverbs 31 woman). That's when it hit me, I had prayed for a man of God, and a Saul had shown up. Saul was described as "a choice and handsome man," and "from his shoulders and up he was taller than any of the people." (1 Samuel 9:16) For this 6'0 tall girl, that seemed like a dream come true, until you look at the content of that towering handsome package. Saul was more concerned about his appearance to the people of Israel than he was serving God, and the result was disastrous. His personal life was also a hot mess. There are numerous parallels between Biblical Saul and this modern-day Saul, whom to date, has gotten a third girl pregnant and is living with an entirely different girl he isn't married to. The poor guy knows the path but can't see through the thorn bushes of his planting. He's a Gomer at heart too. I crave stability and honesty, and his merry-go-round seems exhausting. That's when I got the bright idea to pray for a man like David.

The Bible describes David as "a man after God's own heart." (1 Samuel 13:14) Throughout his life, he chased after God with everything he had, and his love for the Lord is inspiring. This faithful shepherd/poet/warrior's life purpose was worshiping God. How can praying for a man like that go wrong? First of all, he's shorter. Okay fine, that's just 6'0 tall me being superficial. Have I mentioned Bathsheba then? She was the woman David had an adulterous affair with after seeing her bathing on the roof when he should have been off fighting a war. He had her husband murdered to cover up the fact he got her pregnant. I didn't factor that into my prayer equation of trying to strong-arm God into giving me the man I wanted. After the Saul in my life was revealed, my friends went on a mission to find me a David. Mission accomplished because they tried hooking me up with a shorter man who loves the Lord with a self-proclaimed passion that most people in today's day and age don't. However, as I later found out, he was already sleeping with another girl, who had a boyfriend, whom he fought after their love affair was discovered. Thanks, but no thanks. I have enough of my own problems in life without jumping into someone else's love triangle. In hindsight, I think this was an attack from the enemy to keep me separated from his first wife because she is one of my best friends now. Dating this David would have ruined our blooming friendship, and over the years since then, I've seen firsthand what a manipulative narcissist he can be. Once again, I dodged a bullet on that one.

So once again T+G/42= Still no godly husband, which wasn't the desired solution. I buckled down, got specific, and started praying for Boaz. I thought that I indeed had found the one Biblical husband I could pray for that could not end in disaster. Who is Boaz? If you haven't read the book of Ruth, I recommend you stop for a quick second and give it a whirl. It's a teeny tiny book that comes after Judges. It's only four chapters long, so it won't take you long. It's hard to accurately describe such a beautiful love story in a short paragraph, but the main point is that Boaz is Ruth's kinsmen redeemer. He takes this poor foreign widow and shows love, faithfulness, and hesed (חסד)[8] throughout their love story. The word *hesed* shows up three times in the book and is often translated as lovingkindness, grace, and loyal love through actions. It is sacrificial love. It expects nothing and gives selflessly. The entire Bible from Genesis to Revelation points to Christ, and Boaz foreshadows how Christ would redeem us and love us with hesed. Jesus happens to be a direct descendant from the line of Ruth and Boaz. I switched my prayers of David to prayers of Boaz. I mean, this is the type of stuff manipulative prayers are made of! Pure prayer gold baby! Did God send me a Boaz? No, but he sent a Goodfornothingaz Nimrod just to remind me that I can't manipulate Him. God does what He wants.

Although I now agree in hindsight that this man was an "idiot, jerk" like the modern usage of the word, the nickname I gave him in this book is referring to the Biblical character of Nimrod in Genesis 10:10. A descendant of Ham (remember the cursed son from Noah we talked about earlier), he is described as "a mighty hunter before the Lord." Now keep in mind I'm a huntin fool who loves me some time outdoors on the prowl for dinner, so finding a man who shared this passion was a priority. This past summer, I went with a gorgeous group of ladies to an outdoor concert. While there, we ran into one of Johnna's old acquaintances, who had dated her roommate when they were younger. Tall and handsome, he looked like the incredible hulk because he was so muscular. After we left, she asked if I would be interested because he loved hunting and came from a good Christian family. Ugh, duh! She messaged him asking if he was interested, and the next day we started talking. Forget raining men. I'm talking about manly manna from heaven.

He met nine out of ten of the things I was looking for in a man, except for the most important one: a personal relationship with Jesus. I know I come across as judgmental once again, but if you aren't equally yoked, then you aren't playing by the same rule book in a relationship and problems will always arise. It's Biblical. If I'm going to choose to accept the Living Word as my guide throughout life, I also have to accept verses like 2 Corinthians 6:14 which specifically state not to be unequally yoked with unbelievers. This applies to friendships as well as the pursuit of marriage. We become like the people we hang out with most. It's essential as a believer to guard your heart and be intentional about who you allow into your inner circle because over time, you will start to resemble those people. We are not called to be judgmental or ignore nonbelievers. In fact, just the opposite. Christ hung out with sinners regularly but he still had his posse of twelve, and within that twelve, he had three he let in his innermost circle.

One by one, red flags started to appear. Maybe red actually is my favorite color after all. The final straw was when at the tube shoot in New Braunfels, he handed me what appeared to be an icee and told me to take a sip. I swirled it around, and once it got close to my lips, I smelt the alcohol. I asked him if there was alcohol in it, and he said that he wasn't sure but that I was being overly sensitive about it and if I tried harder to overcome my alcoholism that I would be able to drink again. In addition to our numerous talks about the importance of my sobriety, he had family members who also battled addiction, so he wasn't naive on the subject and knew how serious the stakes were for me. This Nimrod had just read an article I had written for the local paper celebrating my three years of sobriety, and here he is trying to kill me that same week. I'm not being dramatic when I say that he was trying to kill me. It is that serious. For the first time in my life, I utilized the block tool, and I haven't looked back. Even if he does love hunting.

During this same time frame, I had gone to Minnesota to celebrate my adorable nephew's first birthday party with my family. On the flight back, I met an incredible girl, who I meet as often as I can for coffee in San Antonio. She messaged me one day that she knew a guy who could be the Boaz I was looking for. Things were wrapping up with Nimrod and she gave him my number. I found out this guy had recently gotten out of a serious long-term relationship, and when he reached out, I told him I didn't think he was ready to date so soon (honestly, I was still finding my bearings too). He said he understood, yet he started sending me devotionals every morning. At 5 am. Recall from chapter one how people texting me this early turns me into a rage monster? Ashamedly I admit I wanted to chuck a clock at this stage five clinger's head. Even after sending him grumpy cat photos and nicely telling him he was texting too early, he persisted. I'm horrible with confrontation, so I slowly started spacing out my response times and not answering phone calls thinking he would get the hint and give up the pursuit. He did not. Clearly, I need to work on confronting people in a loving manner and stop being passive-aggressive. We're all doing our best.

One afternoon, I called one of my best friends to ask her opinion on a different guy who had reached out online (I told you the inner me is a Gomer and ruthless in the pursuit), and she started chewing my a$$ out about my swearing problem. I do admit, I have the mouth of a sailor. My youngest son especially loves to convict me on this issue, and I'm doing my best to stop letting profane crap come out of my mouth. This friend happens to be one of the sweetest women ever and never yells at people, so it felt like a gunshot wound when I was already exhausted and emotionally vulnerable. I sat in my car and started to Kim Kardashian ugly cry. The all too familiar feeling of hopelessness and despair were creeping in, and I couldn't hold it together. I was tired of feeling like a failure and of feeling unloved. Right in the middle of that ridiculous pity party, I got a text message from Stage Five asking me if I was okay. This was an odd time of day for him to text, with it being the middle of the afternoon. Interpreting this interaction as a possible life-saving floatation device thrown at me from God while I was drowning in my tears, I told him that I actually wasn't okay. He asked me if he could call and pray with me. So, he did, and by the end of the phone call, I felt the Holy Spirit's peace and had a softer heart all the way around.

I met Stage Five Samson face to face the first time the next afternoon, and the passion was immediately apparent between our codependent hearts. The first time I saw him, he was running towards me in a military uniform, we embraced, and he prayed over me. Insert romantic music here. We talked about what we were looking for in a marriage, he assured me he was Boaz, and we agreed not to have sex until marriage. It all seemed too good to be true. He booked a ticket for me to accompany him to Saint Lucia (I'm supposed to be there right now as I'm writing this). We started working through a shared Bible plan and memorizing scripture together. The children were all introduced to one another, everyone was happy, and it all seemed too good to be true. It seemed by all appearances that God had parted the "Dating Red Sea" (probably red because of all of my romantic pursuit dreams that had died along the way, if you haven't noticed), yet I knew deep down inside things were moving too fast. The hopeless romantic in me wanted to believe this was the real deal. I mean, he said he was Boaz for crying out loud! Spoiler alert: if a man tells you that he is Boaz, that might be a red flag.

We hit our first argument when he went on a work trip to Houston (the city his recent ex was from), and I sensed an immediate emotional distance in him. I asked him if he was over his ex, and he got defensive. Words were said, I lost my cool and called him a sadistic bastard whose words were meaningless, and he blocked me. Fair enough. Not my finest moment, I agree. Yet somehow, when he reached out a week or two later, I went right back like a moth to a flame. We gave it another shot, I caved and slept with him, and he broke up with me less than twenty-four hours later over dinner. Talk about having the rug ripped out from under you. While looking at the drink menu, he told me that God had at that moment given him a revelation that he needed the evening to be by himself. I suspect it wasn't revelation from the Lord Almighty as much as it was that he wanted alone time so he wouldn't feel guilty for drinking in front of me even though I told him it wouldn't bother me if he did. However, that is speculation, as I'm not telepathic even though I dang sure try to be. Samson had the audacity to ask me to go home but drive the hour back to San Antonio at 5 am because he had something special planned for us. I told him I wasn't a yo-yo and wasn't interested in being strung along back and forth. At that point, he said he realized (after we slept together) that he wasn't over his ex, and we decided to split ways. I say the reason is that he's impulsive, manipulative, and self-centered. That point is moot, and my suspicions are opinion. What I do know is that I was directly disobedient to what God told me, and that was that I needed to stop having sex outside of marriage. I had made it two years celibate before this past summer, and then I went back to my Gomer ways. God wants obedience from his children and will allow discipline in their lives when they aren't listening to Him. I lost my blessing because I didn't follow what I knew he had called me to do as a believer.

A classic vacation bible school favorite, the story of Samson is found in the book of Judges. An angel appeared to his mother before he was born and told her that she would conceive a son, and he would be set apart as a Nazirite. This would mean that throughout his life, he would not drink wine, touch dead things, or cut his hair. As we see in Judges 14-16, Samson would one by one do all three of those prohibited things. We see him partying at his wedding feast for the marriage he was pursuing, one in which he would have been unequally yoked. We watch him eat honey out of the body of a dead lion, which would not be something I would be tempted to do but to each his own. By the time Delilah coaxed the secret for his strength out of him and had his head shaved, it was the final broken straw of his Nazarite vow, and he lost his blessing because of his lifelong pursuit of the flesh and string of poor choices.

A Tabernacle for Me, A Tabernacle for You

It hit me after this breakup that I couldn't hold on to bitterness because we were both a little like Samson inside. This story resonates even more closely with my heart because just like strong man Sam, my mother also had a divine encounter while pregnant. Some of the genetic testing they had done had come back with some false positives. They told my parents that I would have spina bifida and would not have a brain. An abortion was recommended, which was devastating. Thankfully, my mother was a believer, so she prayed and cried to the Lord in anguish, begging for discernment. Suddenly, in one of her darkest moments, she felt the Holy Spirit rush through her like a gust of wind, and from that moment on, she had immediate peace about the decision to not follow through with the recommended abortion. As it turns out, they were wrong about the spina bifida, but the jury is still out on whether or not I have a brain. It is the topic of much debate at family gatherings, and I enjoy the relentless teasing on the subject.

His mother was also a strong woman of faith who had prayed many prayers over her son throughout her life. It was evident in the notes of the Bible she left him when she passed on to be with Jesus forever. We were both chosen before birth. The two of us continue to lose our blessing like Samson did because we both keep succumbing to the flesh. As born-again believers, we are not called to have sex before marriage. This is not because sex is something shameful or dirty. Sex is a beautiful thing. There is something transcending about it, bonding two people's spirits forever. Trust me, I don't have an archaic view of sex; hell-bent on shaming people into submission of Puritan moral beliefs. You can go out and gang bang thirty people on stage in front of a crowd tomorrow and God will love you just as much as he did the day you were born (although I highly recommend against this because there are still consequences for our choices). His love for you has never depended on your actions, good or bad. We aren't called to have a do-it-yourself sense of spirituality. If you put your faith in Jesus, you are in, and nothing you can do will change that except to deny Him.

It says in Judges 14:4 that Samson's parents didn't realize that him chasing a Philistine woman for marriage was actually an opportunity from the Lord against her people. I have full faith and trust that no matter what I do, God can use all of my actions for His good. That being said, I have also had to suffer the consequences of my foolish choices over the years. If I truly love Him, I shouldn't want to continually break his heart trying to fulfill my own selfish desires. He can see the bigger picture when my childish brain can't. Just like a parent sets rules in place so the child doesn't get hurt, there are set guidelines we should follow to avoid future heartbreak.

When we have sex with people, we develop soul ties with them. There is a piece of us that stays with them, and we weren't meant to share that with everyone. It's like the cheesy classic example where someone sticks a piece of clear tape on your skin, and you see the dead skin cells left on the tape. Then if you stick it on another person's arm, it takes away some of their dead skin cells too. Eventually, it loses its stickiness. Same with us as believers. As we pick up soul ties that stay in our hearts, they start to change who we are from the inside out. We are told in 1 Corinthians 6:18 NIV "Flee from sexual immorality. All other sins a person commits are outside the body, but whoever sins sexually, sins against their own body." Your body is the tabernacle of God, and He desires a pure living space to dwell in. Sometimes we mess up and give it up, and there's no shame in that. Already forgiven, we are asked to repent and admit there is a problem and go and sin no more like the adulterous women. (John 8:1-11)

I know this isn't a popular view in today's hypersexualized DTF culture, so once again, I humbly ask you to please not put the book down. As you can see, I continue to struggle in this area, and I come to you in the foxhole not on the pulpit. I'm also preaching to myself here, kids. I thank God for his continued grace. The God of Israel is a God of intimacy, and there just isn't a deep life-giving intimacy found in empty sexual conquests. Sure, it feels damn good in the moment. However, eventually sex without marital intimacy drains the life out of us. We were meant for more than that. We were meant to have life and life abundantly. (John 10:10) We were meant to have one person to walk throughout life with who loves our hearts *and* our bodies, and Christ above all.

Why have I bored you to tears by telling you anything about my romantic pursuits? My point wasn't to make myself Christ-like by comparing myself to the stories of the Bible. This isn't the gospel of Tasha Page. It's all about Jesus. On the same token I do need to point out that "the word of God is living and active, sharper than any two-edged sword, piercing to the division of soul and of spirit, of joints and of marrow, and discerning the thoughts and intentions of the heart." (Hebrews 4:12) If I hadn't made a daily habit of reading my Bible, I wouldn't have been able to recognize when the same sinful patterns of these Biblical giants were also appearing in my life. "What has been is what will be, and what has been done is what will be done, and there is nothing new under the sun." (Ecclesiastes 1:9) None of the desires of the flesh or tricks of the enemy are new. There isn't anything you have done that someone hasn't already thought of before you. Take comfort and strength in knowing that. There is no shame in your past. I love looking at their past stories and discerning how their mistakes can be used to change my future. That is why God gave us the Word. Not to shame us, but rather to give us a lamp to guide our feet. With the Holy Spirit's guidance, jump into this precious gift and ask yourself how the stories within those pages relate to your life. Their stories were important, and so are ours. Your story is unique, given only to you, and is meant to be shared to help others.

At the time I am writing this, I'm in one of those spiritual EKG seasons. I've stopped tripping and falling on penises, and I'm back on track with surrendering to God's will instead of trying to manipulate Him. He's shown me that my insecure anxious attachment style and perfectionism issues are blocking me from having a closer relationship with Him, and need to be addressed before I find a husband. I'm trying to stay in consistent prayer and meditation so that He can fix the broken neurotic parts of my heart. I'm not even looking for Boaz anymore. I realized after Stage Five Samson that Ruth was the one that initiated that relationship and I'm tired of hunting the most dangerous game. The Gomer in me is a man-eater, and I don't have to live like that anymore. For the first time in my life, I am being still, and knowing that God has it all handled. In His timing, if it is His will, He will bring me a Godly man. All I have to do is walk humbly with the Lord my God.

ז

PERFECTIONISM: THE SILENT KILLER

"And now that you don't have to be perfect,
you can be good."
-John Steinbeck

I vividly remember lying in bed as a little girl praying to God with tears streaming down my face night after night, praying to God that he would make me perfect so that I would be worth loving. I still catch myself praying the same prayer at thirty-four at times, even though I know deep down within that I am profoundly loved. Broken parts and all. I sincerely hope that upon the first moment I see Jesus's face that he will squeeze my cheeks, look me in the eyes, and tell me "Girl, you were a hot mess, but I sure as hell loved you." The thought fills my heart with pure joy. Before the Pharisees out there come after me with a pitchfork, I believe Jesus can say "sure as hell" if He wants to because hell is a sure thing.

I have a close friend who also suffers from perfectionism that gets mad at me when I call myself a hot mess, but I think of it as a term of endearment. She is correct when she retorts that our words hold power, reminding me that negative self-talk can be damaging. She asserts that by labeling myself as a hot mess, I am mislabeling my true identity as a daughter of the King of all Kings. However, I like to think that through the transparency of the broken parts of my life, I am able to connect more deeply with others who have the same thorns. I'm all about that kintsugi over here, a Ragamuffin Christian through and through. If you don't know what that term means, I highly recommend reading Brennan Manning's The Ragamuffin Gospel.[1] His target audience is the bedraggled, beat-up, and burnt-out. "It is for the inconsistent, unsteady disciples whose cheese is falling off their cracker." As well as the "smart people who know they are stupid and honest disciples who admit they are scalawags." To all my other Prodigal homies out there, David Leo Shultz also has an excellent movie, similarly titled *Ragamuffin*,[2] which explores the journey to living fully loved in God's grace through the life of Rich Mullins. He's a straight up ragamuffin too, one of the many reasons I love him. His newest movie *God's Fool*[3] is my personal favorite. The man is a creative genius.

Sure, my life is significantly less messy since I decided to surrender it to Christ, but nevertheless, it is far from perfect. Now that I have the sober glow I talked about earlier, I look hotter than ever in my cleaner mess, so the term "hot mess" stays in my vernacular against my friend's wishes. She requested to remain anonymous in this book because she doesn't want people to think badly of her. We both put too much emphasis on what other people think, but hey, we're all doing our best.

Highly Neurotic but Not Psychotic

When I was a teenager, my mom suggested I take a volunteer position so that I would have some experience when I was applying for my first job. One of the few times I wisely took her advice, I happily skipped into the local hospital and was interviewed for a front desk greeter position on the weekends. During that interview, I was asked to give three adjectives to describe myself. Kind, loving, and neurotic were my top three. Wide-eyed, she asked me if I knew what the word neurotic meant, and having only taken one high school Psychology class, I was clearly an expert on the subject. I went into full detail on the definition and how it applied to my circumstances. She shook her head and maternally told me that I should never tell another living soul that. Because of her stern warning, I am naturally more tempted than ever to notify you that I am still neurotic. As a side note, I still got the position, which if you weren't already concerned about the quality of America's healthcare system, maybe you should be now.

Merriam-Webster dictionary lists the essential meaning of neurotic as "often or always fearful or worried about something: tending to worry in a way that is not healthy or reasonable."[4] Related to the word neurosis, those labeled as having a neurotic personality get a bad rap because, on their worst days, these individuals can be moody, pessimistic, and impulsive. While I admit all of these things are at times true, it is said that our weaknesses are often our greatest strengths that need to be channeled in a more positive direction.

A person who shows higher levels of neuroticism may be a more sensitive person to their feelings, social circumstances, and the surrounding physical environment than others.[5] They are often high self-monitors and can adapt to social situations more fluidly as long as they aren't suffering from sensory overload, leading to debilitating anxiety. When channeled in a positive direction, these individuals are excellent listeners, extremely empathic, and have strong levels of intuition. Neurotics and highly sensitive people (HSP) tend to have higher IQ's and greater creativity than their more laid-back counterparts. Because their brains are constantly in overdrive, they tend to develop greater problem-solving skills. What doesn't kill you makes you stronger fo sho.

While it can be frustrating loving the neurotic individual in your life, they just might be the saffron to your salt and just what you need to bust out of autopilot and the daily monotony of life. Similar to authentic saffron, neurotics living their best life have a complex, nuanced flavor with sweet, floral elements to it like empathy, love, and creativity. Imitation saffron has a bitter, metallic taste to it, so whenever there are negative traits like anger, anxiety, and impulsivity being exhibited in your neighborhood neurotic, you can rest assured that the enemy is at work behind the scenes. Pray with them and for them because telling them to stop being so sensitive is never helpful. As the saying goes, "Never in the history of calming down has anyone calmed down by being told to calm down."[6] Recently a fellow neurotic comrade pointed out that whenever she gets stuck in her "crazies," as she calls it, it was beneficial for her to write out a list of how she is feeling versus the facts of the situation. I started implementing this practice in my daily life, and by Jesu it works! I highly recommend the practice to all.

While I might be neurotic, I've learned over the years that I'm not, in fact, psychotic. Crazy people don't realize they are crazy. When my life is dysfunctional, it means that I'm exhibiting harmful paradigms and coping skills I've learned along the way. Famed psychotherapist Carl Jung is quoted as saying "Man is blind to the fact that, with all his rationality and efficiency, he is possessed by 'powers' that are beyond his control. His gods and demons… keep him on the run with restlessness, vague apprehensions, psychological complications, an insatiable need for pills, alcohol, tobacco, food— and above all, a large array of neuroses."[7] I concur, Carl, I concur.

As much as I've prayed for God to remove this thorn of neuroticism, it remains ingrained in the wiring of my soul. This leads me to believe He will use this characteristic for His greater purpose. Throughout my life, I have noticed a trend in that the number one adjective people use to describe me is "sweet." I don't necessarily know if I'm sweet so much as they are unconsciously picking up on the fact that I'm often vividly feeling their underlying emotions and responding empathetically to the best of my ability (Although I don't always discern correctly or respond appropriately). My life is currently in a calm Psalms 23 meadow season, yet I frequently find myself still experiencing anxiety and heightened negative emotions when on the surface, nothing is wrong. I was meditating on the root of this the other day when it hit me that the turmoil, I am currently experiencing is not my own. It's because I'm walking through life with other people who are going through very heavy things right now, and the strong maternal instinct in me is trying to take on their problems as my own.

I'm in the process of surrendering the worries I have for others to God because I don't often have control over my own life, much less theirs. There is an old Hebrew saying, "Let there be such oneness between us that when one cries, the other tastes salt." In Matthew 5:13, Jesus calls us to be the salt of the world, with the implied implication of needing to live a pure life to serve as a "preservative" of the human race to slow down the spiritual decay of the world around them. Sometimes I wonder if my wiring is mixed up, and when others cry, I taste saffron. Either way, at least my story is flavorful.

It's In the Breaking Not the Baking

Momma Duke (aka my mother) recently wrote me a letter I will cherish forever reflecting on Luke 24:13-35.

140

If you aren't familiar with the story, it's about two followers of Christ who unknowingly walked with Jesus on the road to Emmaus. Their eyes were kept from seeing Him as they walked and talked together, discussing their unfulfilled dreams in Christ being the one to redeem Israel. Christ calls them foolish and points them back to the Scriptures, which reveal who He is. As they reach their destination, Jesus pretends that He is going to keep traveling forward, but they urge Him to stay with them instead. Only at the dinner table were their eyes opened, and He made Himself known to them in the breaking of the bread.

The first thing that the men do after they recognize Jesus is rush to find the eleven remaining disciples (and the group that was with them) to tell them about what they had witnessed. They were bursting at the seams to share their testimony because that's what a personal encounter with Christ will do to you. Just like good coffee, Christ is much better when shared with others. He wants us to have rich, full relationships where we share news of the grace and mercy that we have been given as dearly beloved Raggamuffins.

In Momma Duke's letter, she lovingly pointed out that before self-esteem can be the cause of good in our lives, it needs to be the result of our ability to accept the real truth about ourselves. When our self-esteem is poor and we don't love ourselves, we kick Christ in the teeth. We are turning our noses up and scraping them on the ceiling because we think we know better than Him. When we are unnecessarily hard on ourselves, we are implying it's okay not to recognize and cultivate the gifts that He has given us. She reminded me that God trusts me to share His Good News and love to others, and that He has given me all the skills I will need to do it. She asked that I take realistic stock in my abilities and then pray for God's grace and strength to make the rest happen. She pointed out that I already have been given "mad skills," and then she reminded me of her love, and most importantly, God's love for me. If I haven't told you already, Momma Duke is the best.

After dating Stage Five Samson, God spoke into my heart that one of the reasons that our relationship failed was my crippling perfectionism problem. I might or might not have taken Matthew 5:48 out of context when I read: "You therefore must be perfect, as your heavenly Father is perfect." Surely that's a joke, right? I'm not perfect. I will never be perfect in this life. I'm sure you already knew that, but this is a hard pill for my ego to swallow. This unintentional lack of humility is a little foxhole of prideful sin, stemming somewhere from my childhood. It hurts my relationship with Christ and others around me because of my unrealistic demands and relentless struggle for control.

This desire to be perfect originates from the fact we are created in the image of God and were designed to live in a perfect world before sin corrupted it. Amy Baker writes in her book *Picture Perfect*, "Sadly sin has turned what was once a glorious mission into a source of tension. Sin has also caused us to come up with our own definitions of perfection, a man-centered definition that often focuses on performance and outcomes that glorify us, not our creator."[8] Guilty. As. Charged. Thus, I frequently get caught up in my "savior complex" of trying to bake the bread myself rather than sharing the Good News of the bread that was already baked and broken on the cross. In Matthew 26:26, Jesus took the bread, blessed it, and told them "Take and eat; this is my body." When the church gathers together for Communion, it does so in remembrance of what Christ has done for us, using ordinary tangible symbols like bread and wine to symbolize God's covenant fulfilled. It proclaims the goodness of what Jesus accomplished on Calvary and that we need not strive on our own merit because the battle has already been won by the breaking of His body (bread) and His blood (wine) poured out for the forgiveness of your sins. Never once does He tell the disciples to bake the bread themselves. Rather his dying words to us were "Tetelestai" or "It is finished." Taste and see that the Lord is good. (Psalms 34:8)

As a side note, I find it somewhat ironic that I'm gluten intolerant and unable to drink wine because I'm an alcoholic. Maybe that's also another subtle reminder from God that I'm not in control and this world is not my home. Also, I found it very punny with all this talk about bread that God sent me *Picture Perfect* written by Amy (which means beloved) Baker. The "beloved baker's" book was very much needed during this season of life because all of the work-based plans I had been mixing up were a recipe for continuing to make myself and others around me miserable. Her wisdom was such a valuable resource in helping to take a realistic inventory of what makes me rise (or fall). Just like yeast, the sins in our life can ruin a whole batch of bread when it gets out of control. Unregulated perfectionism makes an over-inflated dough that's hard to work with. After a recipe adjustment, I'm back on track. Once again, Momma Duke was right, but don't tell her that.

Riddle Me That, Batman

Being a boy mom of two not so little anymore boys, I have had to become acquainted with the DC Universe if I am to have any hope of understanding what on God's green earth they are talking about the majority of the time. A complex labyrinth of superheroes and supervillains, it's a whole other world living within our world, with elaborate themes that touch on humanity's greatest hopes and fears. The characters are all interconnected in their universe, just as we are in ours, and often show the best and worst traits within a person. Comics over the years divulge their detailed origin stories and tell the background of how these individuals came to be who they are.

One of the characters I find most intriguing is the supervillain The Riddler. He is a criminal mastermind who delights in incorporating puzzles and humorous riddles into his schemes, leaving them as clues to solve his crimes. His birth name is a pun itself, Edward Nigma (enigma-a person or thing that is difficult to understand). In Batman: Legends of the Dark Knight #185-189 the Riddler finds himself powerless and homeless, pushed to the brink of insanity.[9] A chance encounter with a former NSA codebreaker helps him to restore his sanity, and during that encounter, he experiences a flashback that reveals how he came to be the way that he is. Apparently, his father, envious of his son's brilliant mind, accused him of cheating and beat him relentlessly as a child. This discovery leads him to realize that his criminal compulsion for riddles is born out of a strong desire to prove his innocence of deception and to tell the truth. Throughout his life in the DC Universe, he goes back and forth between the urge to do good versus evil.

I suspect what fascinates me most about The Riddler is his obsessive-compulsive desire to achieve his objective, whatever that may be at the moment. Having no special superpowers of his own per se, he relies on his rationale and above-average problem-solving abilities. His greatest weakness is actually his greatest strength being utilized for evil. We discussed in chapter two that what we don't work out we will act out. In The Riddler's case, it was his inability to forgive his father that was at the root of the bitter heart that continued to destroy him one bad decision at a time. Because of this, he couldn't drop the baggage and fully surrender his life for good pursuits. Filtered through the skewed paradigms he acquired growing up, his obsession for domination over the world around him was slowly destroying him from the inside out, resulting in a life of catastrophe.

The neurotic perfectionist within me can relate to the complex internal struggle The Riddler is facing. I often ask myself now that I have been reborn in Christ how I am supposed to do good when my sinful heart is bent on evil? I am driven by the desire to be perfect because I am terrified of the side of myself that has already shown the capacity to do great evil. This fixation repeatedly pushes me to what feels like the brink of insanity, exhibited by manic episodes where I strive my hardest to be perfect and fail, followed by depressive episodes where I completely shut down because it feels like I can't get anything right. Other times, instead of becoming depressed, I throw my hands up and live fully in the flesh, chasing whatever carnal pleasures that are offering even sliver of happiness in front of me. Even in sobriety, it is hard for me to drive in the middle of the road instead of crashing in the bar ditches of abused grace and or unmerciful truth.

I'm slowly coming to terms with the fact that within my soul there is an inner Pharisee that is constantly trying to stone me to death. Recently, I had a good friend slap me out of the blue with the question "Who hurt you so bad?" When my eyes welled up with tears at what seemed like a random question, he pointed out "Everyone around you has already put the stones down. You need to drop the rocks yourself. You don't have to be perfect to be loved." Once again, I saw Jesus, through someone else, hitting me in the head with a two-by-four. I am my own worst critic, and it took the loving harsh words of a kind friend to point out an obvious blind spot in my life. Proverbs 27:5-6 tells us: "Better is open rebuke than hidden love. Faithful are the wounds of a friend; profuse are the kisses of an enemy." Thank God for this man taking a brave risk, even with the potential chance of me reacting badly, by showing selfless Christlike love in pointing out a thorn that was abscessed and couldn't be hidden anymore. He also pranks me on a regular basis, reminding me to lighten up and laugh a little. So grateful for good friends.

Be A Jellyfish

One of the favorite tactics God likes to employ in my life is one I lovingly refer to as the "bait and switch." This means that I often find myself going into a situation thinking I am being sent to accomplish something for God's Kingdom; however, I find out after I get there that He led me there for an entirely different reason. For example, right after I broke up with Jacob, I was in a season of sheer exhaustion from working overnights at one of the local nursing homes as a certified nursing assistant. Despite my weariness, I settled into a rigorous work-based routine while pressing into God more than ever in this season and trying my best to be obedient to hear His will for my life. One evening, I was frantically trying to accomplish as much as possible before I headed into work when the boys asked me to stop what I was doing and watch a movie with them. I kept telling them that I would sit down in a minute, really with no intention of doing so, when at that moment the podcast I was listening to said something about needing to be more intentional about spending time with our kids because if we don't, the enemy will. Feeling convicted, I immediately stopped and sat down with them, thinking that God was going to use this as an opportunity for me to teach them more about who He is during our time together.

The movie was *Galaxy Buck: Mission to Sector 9*.[10] The general overview of the movie is that the main character Buck Denver has a dream to save the galaxy and to spread the word of God's love to every corner of the universe. He has a poster that sits above his cubicle that says "God wants you to do big things". He takes his poster with him and embarks on a journey that eventually finds him in a cave with an Obi-Wan Kenobi type character. Buck starts explaining how he's on a mission to do big things for God, and the Obi guy tears his poster in half so it now says "God wants you" instead. He takes him down into a dark sea cave, shows him these different creatures. Some of them look like sharks, and he explains these creatures never rest, always striving to do things their way. Then he shuts off the lights and they see these jellyfish looking creatures glowing in the dark. Obi explains how the jellyfish drifts from place to place, never striving, yet showing Christ's love wherever it goes. I realized at that moment that God had pulled the bait and switch, and I needed the video more than the kids. My perfectionist sharklike mentality was killing me from the inside out, and destroying my relationships with others. From that day on, the boys and I made a mission statement for our family that says we are "To be a jellyfish in a world full of sharks so that the love of Christ shines through us as we help others drift through the current of life."

I come to you now friend, with love, asking if there is a possibility that you are similarly dying a silent slow death due to perfectionism poisoning the well of your heart? It isn't a coincidence you are reading this book right now. You have been singled out by the creator of the universe to do a favor for God. That favor is to accept the grace that he has offered to you and to live life unconditionally loved as His child with no strings attached. None of your striving or ill-conceived notions of your purpose will suffice here. What you think is perfect falls desperately short of the perfection of God. His ways are not our ways. His thoughts are not our thoughts. (Isaiah 55:8-9) Yet He is more than okay with our inadequacies, and already knew we would have them when He designed us. While your earthly parents might have failed at unconditionally loving you, your heavenly Father is perfect and will stop at nothing to bring you closer to Himself. Even if that means pulling the bait and switch on you too.

ח

Surrounded By Mirrors

"Whatever you may be sure of, be sure of this,
that you are dreadfully like other people."
-James Russell Lowell

As a child, I loved when the carnival rolled into town. As an adult, I perceive them to be portable tents of disgusting overpriced food, unsafe rides, and unobtainable prizes. Tiny Tasha however, saw a temporary wonderland full of possibilities and magical allure. One of the attractions that captivated me the most was the hall of distorting mirrors. If you aren't familiar, these are mirrors that employ curved or tilted surfaces at different angles, which alter the angle at which the reflected light hits your eyes. Some make you appear taller, some wider, and some unrecognizable. It's delightfully disorienting.

Because of their ability to distort reality, they are often used as a literary device. The Snow Queen by Danish author Hans Christian Anderson refers to one known as the "Devil's Mirror" in his classic tale.[1] The devil, in the form of a troll, has made a magic mirror that magnifies the bad and ugly aspects of the object in its reflection. There is a sinister attempt by these evil trolls to take the mirror into heaven to make fools of the angels and God, but their plan fails, and the mirror is sent to the earth, shattering into billions of little pieces, some no larger than a grain of sand. These splinters are blown all over the earth and get into people's hearts and eyes, making them only able to see the bad and ugly in the world around them.

In the very first chapter of the Bible, we are told in Genesis 1:27 "And God created man in His own image, in the image of God He created him; male and female He created them." Do you realize the full significance of that statement? God created us in *His* image. Therefore, I will see glimpses of *Him* in every face I will encounter as I walk this earth. However, in this fallen world, our reality is distorted. Remember, we are all part sinner, saint, and sufferer. When I look at myself and the world around me, I see the world filtered through the devil's mirror in my eyes (and heart) because this world is incapable of perfection.

Good ole Carl Jung was recorded saying "Everything that irritates us about others can lead us to an understanding of ourselves."[2] Once again, I concur, Carl. One of the most popular tricks the devil has used against us is the prideful tendency to think that we are our own individuals who are elevated above, and therefore unlike, the people around us. When I was in rehab, one of the RA's wisely said in passing that if I was being annoyed by the people around me, then I was probably already struggling with the trait that irritated me, and they were only reflecting it back to me. Without knowing it, she gave me an epiphany within my soul that changed my prayer life and the way I see others.

My children are the most significant reflection of the window to my soul in my life. God has a funny way of using them to mimic the character defects within my heart by the behaviors they are exhibiting at the time. For example, my eldest son has a predisposition towards grumbling. When I start to want to sell him on eBay for whining, God convicts me and reveals that he is picking that trait up from me and that I need to get my own heart in line first. So, we pray together about it. My youngest son and I continue to do the same with our anger issues and perfectionism tendencies. By being honest and vulnerable with them, I have allowed them to know I am also human and therefore imperfect. What the devil meant for evil, God has used for good to help us grow together as a family and become closer.

Speaking of mirrors and mimicking, I stumbled across a funny meme the other day that asked, "What color would a chameleon in a room full of mirrors be?" As it turns out, the answer to this question depends on gender. Male chameleons will turn dark shades of red, orange, and yellow, whereas a female will show less subtle color changes or no change at all. Female chameleons aren't yet understood as well as their male counterparts, proving that even across species, some things never change.[3] A person who can adapt to any social environment is commonly referred to as a "chameleon." In the world of psychology, they are referred to as "high self-monitors." People in this category are good at adapting to the situations they are surrounded by and are skilled at getting along with others. On the other hand, "low self-monitors" are less likely to change their behavior to fit in. They are who they are, no matter who is around.

In college, the subject of self-monitoring fascinated me. I would fall on the high self-monitoring side of the spectrum and was curious why I was created this way. As such, my undergraduate research was conducted on this very subject. In 2009, I presented "The Effect of Mimicking and Self-Monitoring on Helping Behavior" at the Midwestern Psychological Association. In my research, participants were led to believe they were taking a revised version of the Thematic Apperception Test and asked to examine twelve photographs with another "student", describing what they saw. What they did not know was that the other student was a fellow researcher (called a confederate). They were placed into separate groups, and some of the participants were mimicked by the confederate and others were not. After the last photograph was shown, the confederate "accidentally" knocked a pencil off the table to see if the participant would pick it up. At the end of the experiment, they were asked to fill out three surveys: 1) one on how they liked the fellow "student," 2) the Snyder Self-Monitoring Scale, and 3) participant information. I found a statistical significance that those who were mimicked, especially those who scored high in self-monitoring, were more likely to be friendly and help the confederate pick up the pencil.

Blind Leading the Blind

In a famous study, psychologists Victoria Horner and Andrew Whiten showed two test subject groups (children and chimpanzees) two mechanical boxes with treats inside them.[4] The first box was opaque, and both groups of test subjects followed the steps the experimenter showed them to obtain the treat from the inside of the bottom of the box. The second box was transparent and showed that the first half of the steps were irrelevant because there was a false ceiling in the box. The human children once again carefully copied all of the steps shown to them by the experimenter. The chimpanzees, on the other hand, did not. They cut to the chase and only performed the actions required to obtain the treat. If you were tempted to blame the children's age for their ignorance, additional research has shown that adults are even more likely to imitate others, even when their actions aren't logical.

Why does this phenomenon take place? What implications does it have in the real world on a grander scale? Evolution theory proposes that the world is such a complex place that no human can learn how to survive unless they follow the step by step trusting of their more experienced elders. In return, theories have suggested that the act of mimicking subconsciously encourages social rapport, inducing fondness between the parties. While I do not believe we evolved from apes, I do think we as a species are constantly evolving. The enemy has plotted Creationism against Evolution when the two things need not be conflicted against one another. Both are possible, but that's a rabbit hole we can discuss on a different day. The main point here is that copying encourages communion.

All this mimicry has its downfalls. There is an old nursery rhyme titled Three Blind Mice.[5] The lyrics are as follows:

> Three blind mice. Three blind mice.
> See how they run. See how they run.
> They all ran after the farmer's wife,
> Who cut off their tails with a carving knife,
> Did you ever see such a sight in all your life,
> As three blind mice?

One could say that escalated quickly. Or did it? Aren't we often doing the same in our daily walks? When we look for happiness and security in others instead of the One our hearts long for, we set ourselves up to be mutilated by the enemy. Sometimes with knives, but more often with hurtful words and actions. Not very many of us live in isolation, so the odds are high we will get hurt at times. The emotions we catch are often contagious. Unless we live firmly rooted in the Word, we act like the blind leading the blind on autopilot for self-destruction. Because of those damn devil mirror shards in our hearts, we cannot love ourselves or others with agape love.

Last year I lost a very dear friend to me. She had been going through a prolonged rough season of her own, and because I was in my own pain, I wasn't able to see her pain. After I got out of rehab, I knew I needed to make amends. I couldn't do them face to face because she lived halfway across the country, and I was barely scraping by working on overnights as a CNA. One night before work, I called her because I felt it in my heart to let her know I was genuinely sorry for all the ways I had hurt her. Our conversation lasted well over an hour, and I was running out of time to get ready for work, so I lied and said I had to go because I had another call coming in. One of many mistakes I made in this friendship, little did I know that she would resent me for that because all she heard was that once again, someone else was more important than she was. Nothing good comes from even a small lie.

She survived a lot that year, picking up the pieces following a breakup she had a massive heart attack in her early thirties, followed by her mother having a heart attack a short time later. This physical manifestation symbolically represented that her heart had incurred too many breaks over the years and couldn't bear it anymore. I recognize this pain because we both struggle with disappointment and loneliness, and I see my reflection in her. We are looking for the love of our lives, and what we desire most consistently eludes us. Break up after breakup, broken friendship after broken friendship; a heart can only do so much before it pushes everyone out. Because I was wrapped up in my own world, as I often am, I hadn't noticed that she hadn't reached out as much lately. I would text her hello with no reply every so often. The last time I reached out, she finally answered, but her response still stabs my heart when I think about it. She said: "F*ck you, and f*ck your Jesus." After dropping that bomb on me, she continued to fire shots, releasing resentments she had piled up for years. She was mad I hadn't flown up to see her after her heart attack, not seeing my perspective that I no longer had the finances to do so because I no longer had a sugar daddy and was trying to live a more ethical lifestyle. She threw that back in my face when I tried to defend myself, telling me that if it was another vacation that I was after, I would have no problem sucking a couple dicks to get there. She told me not to contact her again until I apologized to her face for not being who she wanted me to be.

Her words still break my heart. I know I have wronged her, but I can't change the past. What breaks my heart most about the loss of this friendship is how lost she is. Admittedly, part of the reason I kept myself at a distance from her was that I knew our friendship was toxic in many ways because we were both two broken people desperately clutching for any relief from the pain in our lives. Once I got sober and mentally healthier, the distance between the two of us grew because I pulled back to learn how to stay afloat. As any lifeguard will tell you, when a person is drowning, the instinctive drowning response kicks in, suppressing rational behavior as seen in the person flailing around manically clutching at anything that could pull them out. She is still drowning, and my survival depends on not getting pulled back into the dark waters of addiction. There hasn't been a day that has gone by that I haven't thought of her and prayed she would find God and relief from the demons she is being tormented by. I can't save her, and never could. I can only forgive her for the hurtful things she has said and pray that she will one day do the same for me.

Love Your Neighbor as Yourself

Frederick Buechner, in his work *Telling Secrets*, reminds us that "None of us has the power to change other human beings like that, and it would be a terrible power if we did, the power to violate the humanity of others even for their own good."[6] As seen above, it is excruciating to see someone heading down the path of self-destruction and not being able to do anything about it. I want to shake her (and many other people I know) and tell her how loved she truly is. I want to tell her she is the daughter of the most high King and that she doesn't have to drown in pain anymore. That's when it hits me that God probably feels the same way about me too. He watches me, wanting to shake me while His heart breaks when I don't love myself.

In Mark 12:28-34, a scribe asked Jesus which commandment was the most important. Jesus answered, "The most important is, 'Hear, O Israel: The Lord our God, the Lord is one. And you shall love the

Lord your God with all your heart and with all your soul and with all your mind and with all your strength.' The second is this: 'You shall love your neighbor as yourself.' There is no other commandment greater than these." First and foremost, it is essential to note that Jesus pointed the man right to God. He is what our hearts need above all things. Secondly, it is important to note that he used His own Word by quoting Deuteronomy 6:5. He often responded to questions by using scripture because His Word is the truth, and the enemy can't defeat it. Finally, the reason I brought this scripture up was to point out that He said "You shall love your neighbor as yourself."

Most of the time, when we hear this, the takeaway is that we should show more love to those around us. A magnificent goal indeed. What we often fail to notice is the last part: *As yourself*. We are called to love ourselves because without self-love, we cannot truly love anyone else. If you are drowning in your self-hatred, you cannot throw someone else a life preserver. Buechner hits the nail on the head when he says "Love yourself not in some egocentric, self-serving sense but love yourself the way you would love your friend in the sense of taking care of yourself, nourishing yourself, trying to understand, comfort, strengthen yourself."[6]

How well are you taking care of yourself? Your body is your temple. It is where the Spirit of God dwells within you. He wants our temples restored. In *Walking With God*, John Eldredge says "All of the things we long for in life- love and friendship, freedom and wholeness, clarity of purpose, all the joy we long for- it depends on our restoration. You can't find or keep good friends while you are still an irritating person to be around. And there is no way love can flourish while you are still controlling. You can't find your real purpose in life while you're still slavishly serving other people's expectations of you. You can't find peace while you are ruled by fear. You can't enjoy what you have while you're envying what the other guy has. On and on it goes. God wants us to be happy. Really. 'I have come that they might have life, and have it to the full.' (John 10:10) But he knows that in order for us to be truly happy, we have to be whole. Another word for that is *holy*. We have to be restored."[7] The word holy in Latin is *sanctus*. It is where we get the word "saint" from. The Proto-Indo-European root of sanctus is *san*, which means "healthy, happy."[8] He wants this for all of His saints, and all who are one with Christ are saints. (Colossians 1:26)

Never let someone tell you that you aren't a saint. You might not be perfect, but if you have accepted Christ into your heart, Christ's blood makes you righteous and holy. It isn't a matter of egotistically rejecting other religions based on exclusivity or superiority. It is a matter of accepting that we all sin and fall short of the glory of God. (Romans 3:23) Because even the most innocent of us sin, we are unable to stand in front of a perfect and spotless God because He can't be in the presence of sin. (Habakkuk 1:13) Sin requires a sacrifice. God loved us so much that He sent His only Son as that sacrifice, and all who believe will have eternal life with Him. (John 3:16) All other world religions expect you to do good works to earn your way into heaven. Only Christianity sent God to you, to find a way to bring you back to Himself, because none of us can stop sinning. Don't beat yourself up about it, just accept the gift of salvation. For it is said "The righteous shall live by his faith." (Habakkuk 2:4)

I Must "Axe" You a Question

I recently took a trip back to my small hometown in central Florida. It had been over fifteen years since I had been home, and I was dying to see how much things had changed. I am one of the only ones in our entire group of girls that no longer lives there. This trip was prompted because one of my girlfriends had found some of our old home movies we had filmed on VHS. Upon my arrival, our original crew gathered together and we had a pajama party and watched (to our horror) the movies we had made in our preteen years. Let's just say all the video evidence has now been destroyed, and some things you just can't unsee. One of the most painful parts of our viewing experience was watching a twelve-year-old version of myself trying to twerk (before twerking was common vernacular). Knowing that I was failing miserably, I walked right up to the camera and said "I have no idea what I am doing". I still feel like that most of the time to be honest, and I still can't twerk to save my life. Some things never change.

Other than catching up with my girlfriends, my favorite part of the trip was having them drive me around, filling me in on the last fifteen years and showing me all the things that had changed over the years. Except for the Roller Barn. That looked exactly the same. I'm pretty sure they haven't even changed a lightbulb in that place, and the thought of all the bodily fluids in the carpets scares me (I'm not even super germaphobic either). One of the things that broke my heart was the deterioration of the local mall. It's once bright white circus tent canopy that covered the food court was now covered in mold. All the major department stores had closed down, and the former Kmart was now a local axe throwing place. The man with the mullet who owned it was proud to tell me that he would be installing an indoor go-kart track next. With all the jokes I had made about my childhood local mall being a circus, now it is literally turning into one. This inadvertently proves the power of our words, so be careful what you speak into existence kids. It felt like my childhood had died.

On that trip I realized that Florida was no longer home anymore, although I still have people I love dearly there. Although most of my circle of friends have made their way out of the pit, I realized that the majority of the people I grew up with did not. Many are fellow addicts/alcoholics, but they haven't found freedom and are stuck in their own versions of hell. The girls told me story after story of people who had been sentenced to prison, others living in abusive relationships, and some who had already died. I realized that it was an incredible gift that God had pulled me out of there when I was fifteen and moved me to Minnesota (and then to Texas when I was twenty-four). Had I stayed in Florida, I most likely would have ended up pregnant with Depeche's baby as a teenager and had a much rougher life than the one He has given me. A few of my friends did have teenage pregnancies, and I'm so proud to see how much they fought and persevered. These fierce women raised some awesome girls of their own. Through talking with the girls, I was able to piece together many forgotten parts of my past and to more fully understand the foundation my life is built on.

We've reached the point where I must "axe" you a question or two. What is your foundation built on? We already examined our households in chapter two, but go deeper and look at the culture you grew up in. How did the accepted beliefs and cultural norms shape your current paradigms? What traits of yours do you see in those around you, and what traits of theirs do you see in your own reflection? Motivational speaker Jim Rohn has a theory that we are the average of the five people we hang out with most.[9] Bust out a pen and a notepad and take some time to ask yourself what traits the five people in your inner circle are exhibiting, good and bad. Are these traits you want to encourage in yourself? Write out a list of nonnegotiables for what a person in your inner circle must have. For example, if you value trustworthiness most, and one of your closest friends is a massive gossiper, ask yourself if this is someone you want to slowly become like? As discussed earlier, often without realizing it we slowly start to mimic the behaviors of those around us. By having a list of nonnegotiable values for friendships (and potential marital partners for my fellow single friends out there), we are more equipped to surround ourselves with people who will help us grow instead of people who want to pull us down into the pit with themselves. We don't have to completely remove people who don't meet the criteria on our lists from our lives, but we should guard our hearts more carefully around them.

I like the NLT version of Proverbs 4:23 which says, "Guard your heart above all else, for it determines the course of your life." I have a tattoo of a big lock and key and this verse on the top of my foot. Even though I got the tattoo three years ago, it still hurts from time to time. I was telling this to someone and they pointed out that maybe the reason it is still tender was that I still wasn't very good at guarding my heart. Perhaps it's time to perform yet another spiritual EKG and ask God what (or who) needs to change in my life. Don't be afraid to do this yourself, for the truth sets us free.

ט

Unwanted Gifts

"I came naked from my mother's womb,
and I will be naked when I leave.
The Lord gave me what I had,
and the Lord has taken it away.
Praise the name of the Lord!"
-Job 1:21 NLT

Hippopotomonstrosesquippedaliophobia

Depending on your life experiences, the word above incited confusion, laughter, or fear. Ironically, it is the word for "fear of really long words".[1] Whoever came up with the name must have been a sadistic evil genius. They can come sit at my table anytime. Let's break this down though. What feeling did the word give you when you read it the first time? What feeling do you have about it now? The fact is, that it is only a word. It's how you perceive it that makes all the difference.

Google's definition of fear is "an unpleasant emotion caused by the belief that someone or something is dangerous, likely to cause pain, or a threat." Looky there, fear is an *emotion*. The definition of emotion is "a natural instinctive state of mind deriving from one's circumstances, mood, or relationships with others." Now we are cooking with hot oil! If fear is an emotion deriving from one's circumstances, then it lies to reason that in order to overcome fear, we need to change our circumstances (internal or external). The battlefield is actually our state of mind. Fear is the body's way of shouting to us that something is wrong. It is a gift from God, to peer into the window of your soul to see that your faith has been placed in the wrong things. It might be an unwanted gift in the moment you are experiencing it, but it is still a gift nonetheless. You can't fix a problem that you aren't aware of. Worry is worshiping the problem. Prayer is surrendering the problem to the one that can fix it.

I can hear it now, some of you might be thinking "okay Einstein, that's much easier said than done. I've prayed countless times and I still can't get out of this cycle of panic." You aren't alone. According to the Anxiety & Depression Association of America (ADAA),[2] over forty million adults over the age of eighteen have been diagnosed with an anxiety disorder, which is 18.1% of the population. These disorders develop from a complex set of risk factors, which includes genetics, brain chemistry, personality, and life events. Although there isn't one underlying cause, there is one underlying solution: faith. Jesus is quoted on many different occasions, after healing people from various ailments, that it was their faith that made them well. (Matthew 9:22, Mark 5:34, Luke 17:19) He was constantly pointing out the connection between faith and healing. That being said, head knowledge is much different from heart knowledge. Andrew Bennett once wisely said: "The longest journey you will ever take is the 18 inches from your head to your heart."[3]

Wrangling the heart into submission is challenging. The heart wants what the heart wants. Billy Graham cut straight to the point when he said, "Anxiety is the natural state when our hopes are centered in anything short of God and his will for us."[4] It all goes back to that obsession we have with domination over our little worlds. When we get off the Lord's throne and give Him control again, He can do great miracles. What is a person to do when they have little faith? That's never been an issue for God. He tells us that faith, even as small as a mustard seed, can move mountains. (Matthew 17:20) What if rallying up that much faith seems impossible? Pray about it. Don't believe me? What else do you have to lose? You don't have to summon the strength to believe His truth on your own. Faith is a gift from above, for "For by grace you have been saved through faith. And this is not your own doing; it is the gift of God." (Ephesians 2:8) Did you catch that? Fear might be a gift, but faith is also a gift. He tells us in the following verses that faith is gifted to keep us from self-righteously bragging about our works. We are *His* masterpiece, in Christ, created for works that *He* designed us for long ago. If He can intricately design an entire universe, surely He can increase your faith if you ask Him. You have to ask, though. Your free will is also a gift, and remember, God is a gentleman not a rapist.

169

Ophidiophobia

If you hadn't noticed, the number for this chapter is the letter ט, one of the two Hebrew letters for "T" we talked about in chapter two. It has a paleo meaning of "snake." As a little girl, I wasn't afraid of snakes any more than your average Jane. However, after thirty-four years of attacks from our enemy introduced in Genesis 3, I have an entirely different perspective on the crafty creature. That snake will stop at nothing to poison God's children. On my better days, my faith holds me up, and there isn't much I fear. Yet most days, I'm a modern-day Israelite, and my emotions tend to get the best of me more often than I would like to admit. My heart often forgets all the miracles I've already seen thus far in my journey, and the dangers my God has already delivered me from along the way.

In Gavin De Becker's life-changing book, *The Gift of Fear*,[5] he talks about fear being a gift to protect ourselves from danger. He shatters the myth that violent acts are unpredictable and teaches us to trust our gut instincts to learn to recognize patterns and behaviors meant to harm us. He credits his violent, traumatic past as the key to his success in helping teach others to overcome their fear. He declares, "It turns out I was attending an academy of sorts, and though hopefully on different subjects, so were you. No matter what your major, you too have been studying people for a long time, carefully developing theories and strategies to predict what they might do." He goes on to say that even in the most despised among us, there are reflections of ourselves. When we learn to accept our own flawed humanity, we are more likely to recognize the harmful predators among us because we silence the voices of denial that tell us, 'That person doesn't look like they will hurt me." Never forget that the human heart is the most deceitful of all things and desperately wicked. (Jeremiah 17:9) I don't bring this up to be pessimistic about humanity. When we accept this to be true, we can objectively look for destructive patterns in our daily interactions because we aren't living naively anymore.

The hopeless romantic in me wants to trust that people are good inside and aren't selfishly motivated. While I do believe that the majority of us do have relatively good hearts, there is still a tiny monster lurking within each and every one of us. In my autopilot moments, I forget this and walk naively into situations without guarding my heart. Once in high school, I noticed a friend looking upwards for an abnormally long time. I asked him what he was staring at, and he replied "someone wrote gullible on the ceiling." Naturally, I looked. I would probably still do the same today, as I tend to be naturally trusting of people. Living with an open heart isn't a bad thing, as long as you are continually praying for discernment.

The world's definition of discernment is the ability to judge well. From a Christian perspective, it is a God-driven process in which an individual discovers something that can lead to future action. The ability to discern is one of the gifts of the Holy Spirit that Paul talks about in 1 Corinthians 12. Other gifts he mentions in this section are the gifts of wise advice, healing, the ability to perform miracles, prophesy, and *faith*. Yes, you read that correctly. Did you catch that? Paul confirms once again that faith is a gift. Like any gift, we can't demand it. We can only pray for it and come back with gratitude when we receive it. The Holy Spirit distributes all of these gifts to all believers how He sees fit. Depending on your purpose for the Kingdom, He might give you one gift more than another in a season of life if it will enable you to fulfill your mission at that particular time.

Often the most misunderstood member of the Trinity, the Holy Spirit is a person, not a ghost prowling around waiting to pop up when you least expect it. However, He can be pretty sneaky in how He goes about changing the hearts and lives of the believer. He's the one responsible for all the "bait and switches" in my life. My heart leaps for joy when I think of my Ruach HaKodesh. I don't know if it's blasphemous to say that He's my favorite part of the Trinity considering all that Jesus suffered, but I'm drawn to the Spirit's exciting personality the most out of the three. He is mysterious, elusive, powerful, convicting, full of life and breath. He's referred to numerous times as "the helper." (John 14:16-18, Romans 8:26) I don't think it's accidental that Matthew 3:16 (when God gave Jesus the Holy Spirit as his helper) and John 3:16 (when God gave Jesus to us as our help towards finding eternal life) are both verses that show us where our help comes from. I would argue 2 Timothy 3:16 falls into that category also by declaring "All Scripture is inspired by God and is useful to teach us what is true and make us realize what is wrong in our lives." We need all the help we can get because this life is often painful. I don't know how I survived life without the Holy Spirit. It's comparable to trying to drive a car with no fuel.

Hidden Grace

The name Job has become synonymous with suffering. Found in the middle of the Old Testament, Job is credited with being the oldest book in the Bible chronologically. It is part of a small subsection of books referred to as the "wisdom literature." In many ways it goes hand in hand with Revelation, the last book found in the New Testament. It's noteworthy that both books mention satan by name, which is rare throughout the entire 66 books of the Bible. If we look at God's story chronologically, the beginning shows satans agenda to destroy God's children, then the end reveals his fiery fate for doing so.

An incredible book, Job explores the concept of grace more than any book in the Old Testament, in my opinion. Christians define grace as "unmerited favor." We see in chapter one that God calls Job "a blameless and upright man, who fears God and turns away from evil." It would stand to reason that if we had a works-based God, He would have denied satan permission to test Job's faith by taking away everything worldly he cherished because he didn't sin to deserve such a cruel fate. Instead, we see living proof that horrible circumstances are not always directly caused by sin. Bad things do happen to good people, and when they do it's not an indication that we deserve them or that God doesn't love us.

God allowed these trials to test Job, possibly to strip him of his hidden self-righteousness. By chapter 37, we see Job crying out to God in criticism and angst, with a judgmental heart. He starts to ask God "Where are you? What are you doing?" Yet, he was still referred to as "blameless." Job is only righteous because God says he is, and what God speaks comes true. Remember the story of Gideon in Judges 6 where the angel of the Lord (aka the preeminent Christ) refers to him as a "mighty man of valor" even though by appearances, he wasn't one at the time because he had yet to lead a battle? Yet God said it, and lo and behold, it came true. Gideon became a fierce warrior who was even listed as a hero in Hebrews 11 Hall of Faith. Ultimately, these two stories don't tell us as much about the characters themselves as they do the gracious nature of God. The Lord allowed the gift of pain in Job's life knowing the outcome would bring Him in right relationship with Himself, and He will stop at nothing to do the same for us because He loves us and desires intimacy. In the end, Job received a double blessing, not because he earned it but because our good God wanted to give it.

Are We There Yet?

As a mother to two little boys, I've grown accustomed to hearing the words "Are we there yet?" Every time they ask me, it makes me smile because I look around and know that we aren't. I'm sure ready for Jesus to come back though. Last Sunday, Pastor Ed at CBC mentioned the concept of being "heresick" because we've never actually seen "home" yet. That is the word I've been searching for my whole life. Heresick. The older I get, the more things on my body are starting to hurt. My earthly tabernacle is deteriorating. In her book *Living Between Alpha & Omega*, author Stella Zuniga Burkhalter says "Our earthly bodies are like tents, flimsy and perishable. We are uncomfortable in these tents, groaning in pain. When we are resurrected, though, our bodies will be like permanent homes, glorified and perfected in ways we cannot imagine (2 Corinthians 5)."[6] I can't wait! I suppose I will have to until He decides it's time though.

Does all this pain have a purpose? The longer I live, the more I start to see the Creator's intentionality for this often-unwanted gift. Pain is like a megaphone shouting into our souls that something is wrong. It shouldn't be ignored. Philip Yancey, in his life-changing work *Where Is God When It Hurts?* explores the purpose of pain in our lives. He points out that "Too often the emotional trauma of intense pain blinds us to its inherent value."[7] He points to Dr. Brand's work with leprosy, the world's oldest disease, which shuts off the pain sensors in its victims. For years it was thought that the disease itself caused the disfigurement in those afflicted, but he disproved that theory. He discovered that because the patients could not feel pain, they were more likely to continue daily activities that were harmful to their well-being. These injuries were likely to get infected, causing severe abnormalities.

Dr. Brand received a several million-dollar grant to design an artificial pain system. He successfully did so, but the experiment didn't turn out as they hoped. The systems were expensive, prone to mechanical breakdown, and likely to be ignored by the patients unless the signals were out of reach. First, they tried an audible system, but the patients would turn the alarm off and continue the dangerous task at hand. Then they tried blinking lights, but those were just as likely to be dismissed. Finally, they resorted to electric shock, but even that wasn't enough for the patients who couldn't feel the pain to stop hurting themselves. By the end of the experiment, his takeaway was "I remember thinking how wise God must have been in putting pain out of reach."

How often do we do this in our own lives? I had to hit my own personal rock bottom before I was willing to turn my life over to God. I had numbed myself with painkillers, drugs, and alcohol for so long that I didn't even realize that what I needed most was missing: God. Although I didn't see it this way at the time, all of the pain I went through was a gift because I wouldn't trade the intimacy I have now with the Lord for anything in the entire world. I credit the ability to use pain for personal growth as one of the key reasons I have been able to stay sober and find serenity. The majority of the time, I don't ignore the alarm anymore, and I'm slowly getting better about not even grumbling about it. Day by day, I pray and turn my life over to Him, and He constantly shows up. After a while, I started noticing Him in most things. If you look for Him, you will find Him. I keep my eyes on Christ and press on towards Him. "Not that I have already obtained this or that I am already perfect, but I press on to make it my own, because Christ Jesus has made me His own." (Philippians 3:12)

There is always the possibility that there is another dark night of the soul season around the bend, but throughout the good times and the bad, I now try to be like Brother Lawrence and have a constant stream of communication with God at all times. We talked about his book *The Practice of the Presence of God*[8] in chapter one, and if you haven't read it yet, please do as it will completely change your relationship with God. It has helped me view prayer as an ongoing conversation with Jesus instead of a stoic obligatory act before meals and bedtime. I have had enough experiences walking with Jesus that there is no doubt in my mind He is my savior. I write these things down and store them in my heart to pull out when the bad times hit, and I don't have the strength to go on. Even if He never blessed me with another thing, I've been blessed beyond measure because I have Him now. I sincerely pray you experience the joy that comes from a relationship with Christ also.

No Weapon Shall Prosper

I absolutely love Psalm 121:1-2, "I lift up my eyes to the hills. From where does my help come? My help comes from the Lord, who made heaven and earth." King David wrote these words as he was standing from the perspective of the palace as he was looking out towards all of the mountainous terrain he had crawled through as Saul tried to kill him. He battled daily for many years even after being anointed because the closer you walk with God, the bigger the bounty the enemy places on your head. God's words over his life came to pass, but it was in God's timing, not David's. He eventually was promoted to the palace once God knew he was strong enough to handle the blessing.

Standing where I am today, I can see many of the hills and caves that satan tried to kill me in throughout the years. I had already developed ulcers and other digestive issues by the age of twelve because of my inability to handle my emotions appropriately. As the years passed, I developed worse coping techniques, which evolved into my various addictions. As we've already discussed, I still battle with depression and anxiety from time to time, but now they are more like familiar acquaintances when they show up rather than my best friends. I still struggle with self-esteem issues, and it is a challenge each time I look in the mirror to think anything positive even though I have been told I am beautiful. I see how I've been delivered from my past hills, and I surrender my spirit to Him as He works on removing me from others. It's given me a whole new appreciation for the strength in my scars. I'm a fierce warrior, and each scar is a reminder that satan lost that battle.

Anxiety and pain are normal parts of the human experience, so God, in His wisdom, gave us the tools we would need to combat these weapons used against us by the enemy. I can't stress the importance of getting in the Word. We've turned into a culture that can't be bothered to read. Therefore, we have laid our swords down, asking the enemy to devour us. We are called to put on the whole armor of God so we can stand against the schemes of the devil. (Ephesians 6:10-20) Your faith is your shield, and His Word is your sword. When we take the time to store His Word in our hearts, the Holy Spirit can help us recall these weapons when we need them most. As you wield your sword, remember not to stab people with it as the Pharisees did. God's Word should be spoken with grace and truth, not used to hack your brother's ear off. Let the Holy Spirit do the convicting in someone else's life. I promise you that if you spend even 10 minutes in the Word every morning, you will start to see unbelievable miracles. You wouldn't eat food only once a week. Comparably your Spirit needs to be fed numerous times a day with God's Truth.

Another major weapon God has given us is the Sabbath. This concept is misunderstood as laziness in our high-strung works-based culture, but it is actually a command from God. Found in the Ten Commandments in Exodus 20:8-11, we are directly commanded to refrain from work one day a week and concentrate on loving God. God made heaven and earth in six days and rested on the seventh as a template for us to do the same. When we work nonstop, we exhibit our pride and show God that our goals for world domination are more important than loving Him. If you hadn't noticed throughout the entire Old Testament, God doesn't do well with idolatry. He demands to be first in our lives. What alarm signals are going off in your life? Are you hitting the snooze button on your sabbath time? Are you stopping to ask God the root of your problems?

Let's say you are spending time with God reading/meditating on your Bible, praying, and sabbathing but are still plagued by fear, pain, and anxiety. I want to say very clearly that there is no shame whatsoever in seeking a medical professional for help. I've been very open and candid about my usage of counseling throughout the years. I genuinely think everyone should use this tool because we all face battles bigger than ourselves and need help with discernment. I've tried almost every antidepressant out there without success, but I've had many friends who had much better luck than I did with them. Our brains are a physical organ, and sometimes they need medical help getting their chemistry back into balance. There is no shame in this! Don't listen to a bunch of Pharisees above what God tells you is right for you. Everybody's journey is different, and we all need various tools to get to the destinations that God has planned for us.

More than anything, I feel like God is refining my heart to a humbler position. "Humble yourselves, therefore, under the mighty hand of God so that at the proper time He may exalt you, casting all your anxieties on Him, because He cares for you." (1 Peter 5:6-7) It's the Micah 6:8 lifestyle I've been called to. When I get off His throne, He always steps in and calms the storms in my life. It's when I think I can do things better than He can that my anxiety kicks into overdrive. His way has always turned out to be better than my way. When I let go and trust He will save me, He has always used every bad situation for good. No matter what the enemy tries to throw at me, no weapon shall prosper. Do you know how I know this? The Word tells me so. (Isaiah 54:17) And God's Word never fails. Ask Job.

Every day, I am coauthoring my life story with God. Like any good father, He delights in reading the story I have written so far. The mountaintop moments make Him jump with joy, and the sad scenes rip His heart out. However, every book needs a good editor to point out mistakes that have been made or suggestions for improving the storyline. If I decide to hold onto the pen, refusing to let it go to editing, I'm limiting my life story's potential for greatness. When I turn the pen over to the One who knows and sees all, oh the places I'll go! Who is holding the pen to your story? You can often tell who has a grip on the pen by looking at how your story makes you feel. Do you have a deeply rooted inner peace that comes from the Prince of Peace? Are you lying down in green pastures of your mind even while the storm rages outside? Are you running from cave to cave in terror, unsure of where your help comes from? Only you have the free will to write how the main character will react to the circumstances, whatever they may be. And only you have the free will to turn that pen over to our loving Editor if you don't like how your story makes you feel. Let go of the pen.

׳

PHARISECTOMY

"Yet what people fail to understand is this:
Christianity is not a message;
It's a lifestyle.
It's caught, not taught."
-Peter Haas

I have an old soul. Although I am technically a
Millennial by birth year, I am more like a Generation
Xer at heart. The anthem for my teenage years was
Smells Like Teen Spirit by Kurt Cobain. The song's
lyrics have a nihilistic vibe ("With the lights out, it's
less dangerous. Here we are now, entertain us. I feel
stupid and contagious"[1]) and were the anthem for my
apathetic and cynical teenage years. The instant the
notes hit my ears; they take me back to where I was
when I fell in love with the song. Music has a way of
connecting with the soul that is unexplainable, only
felt. Detriggering music from my addictive urges was
one of the most challenging processes of recovery, one
that I still grapple with today. Within seconds, a few
melodic notes can change my mood and trajectory for
the entire day for good (or bad if I'm not careful). Like
a tiny virus picked up on a shopping cart, music is
contagious and can impact us forever.

Through a mixture of your genetic wiring and your individual collective life experiences, you are predispositioned to becoming "infected" by particular songs. Then once you are exposed to the song (perhaps by a friend, social media or happenstance), it allows its lyrical DNA/RNA to go straight to the nucleus of your heart and soul. If your immune system doesn't fight it off, it will replicate, and you will want to listen to the song more frequently, exposing others in the process. As good viruses help support our immune systems, there are incredible songs that give us the wind beneath our wings. Still on the fence about you, Bette Midler. I'm torn between that golden lyrical content and the awful 80's cheesiness. Either way, your musical infection made quite a mark on many hearts.

Books are the same as music in that they also have the ability to transfer their content into the nucleus of our hearts. One of my favorite authors is C.S. Lewis. Former atheist, he went on to become one of the most celebrated Christian authors of the twentieth century. I'm torn between *The Screwtape Letters* and *The Great Divorce* as my favorite work of his, but I suppose it depends on my mood. His book *Mere Christianity*[2] discusses the fundamental tenets of Christianity and is an excellent read aimed at sensible skeptics to prove that God does exist. The section "Good Infection" talks about how all things in life are "caught." He goes on to say that the whole offer that Christianity makes is that if we let God have his way with us and accept that Christ is the Son of God, then we can also be sons of God. He promises that: "We shall love the Father as He does and the Holy Ghost will arise in us. He came to this world and became a man in order to spread to other men the kind of life He has- by what I call 'good infection.' Every Christian is to become a little Christ." That's it. That's the entire goal of Christianity. Becoming Christ-like. It's when we take our eyes off that, we become Pharisees.

Babbling Believers

What is the difference between a Pharisee and a Sadducee? The Sadducees didn't believe in the afterlife, so they were *sad-you-see*. Ba dum tss. But really, who are these two groups frequently mentioned in the New Testament? They were both Jewish sects during Jesus's day known for their strict observance of the rules and ceremonies of the Torah. Unlike the Sadducees who only followed the written law, the Pharisees also included oral traditions, the belief of heaven/ hell, and angels/demons. They will forever go down in history as the factions so focused on working their way to God that they somehow missed that He was standing right in front of them. Jesus constantly had to call them out on their misguided notions, and in return, they started plotting how to get rid of Him. God allowed their ignorant actions to be used for His greater plan, and Christ was crucified on Calvary. Afterward, they bribed the soldiers to lie and say the disciples came and stole the body so that the truth of the resurrection wouldn't spread. (Matthew 28:11-13) Jerks. Who does stuff like that? You do. As do I. We all have a little Pharisee in us.

This isn't a black or a white issue, but more of a spectrum. To answer where you lie on that spectrum, the questions must be answered, "Do you believe that God came to earth as Jesus Christ, out of His unconditional love and grace, because we couldn't work our way to Him? How much do you believe His grace is enough?" How you answer those questions reveals your location on the scale. If the answer is not at all, we need to have a totally different conversation. But for argument's sake, let's say you already have accepted Christ as your Lord and Savior. We'll put you at the liberal left if you believe that the following are mandatory to be a Christian: Missionary work, evangelism, speaking in tongues, casting out demons, etc. On the flip side, we will put you on the conservative right if you believe the following are mandatory: designated prayer times, memorizing Bible scriptures, church attendance, tithing, volunteering, etc. While all of these things are good, they aren't God. God is found only at the center of the spectrum, hanging on Calvary, asking you personally if His grace is enough. Everything else is legalistic and, in essence, was the root of the Pharisee's problem. They were so hyper focused on doing all the right things that they took their focus off God. They were all truth and little grace. That bird can't fly far.

If we want to be honest about it, somewhere deep within all of us the deal seems too good to be true. It doesn't seem like a fair transaction to accept His gift without earning it. We make our own lists of things that we need to do to work towards growing closer to

Christ. As man found out at the Tower of Babel in Genesis 11, we can't work our way up to God; it is He who comes down to us. When works-based activities divert our attention away from the relentless grace shown on Calvary to bring our death-destined souls back to Him, then it leads to a babbling believer. You might be asking yourself what in tarnation is that? I never thought you would ask. A babbling believer is one that talks in an incomprehensible legalistic language without guidance from the Holy Spirit. An example of this would be a person trying to shove complicated doctrine down a nonbeliever or a spiritually immature Christians' throat like Paul refers to in 1 Corinthians 3:1-3. If a person hasn't come to terms with the basic message of the Gospel that Jesus loved them enough to die for their sins, then all the rest of it is steak.

The Pharisees had babbling believing down to a science. They were loud and proud, not afraid to jump on anyone like a spider monkey if they even thought about questioning the system. Their legalism wasn't Spirit-filled, so it missed the mark completely. Sin is anything that misses the mark of God's holy perfection. In all their striving toward perfection, they were as sinful as everyone else. Many churches are filled with modern-day Pharisees, who insist that the members of their denomination adhere to *their* preferred language/cultural requirements to fit in. Followers are given a specific list of X, Y, and Z. When believers deviate from the established guidelines, they are often shamed, kicked out, and sometimes decide to leave the church forever.

Anything that pushes people away from Christ makes me want to flip tables. Let's throwback to the '90s, dig out our bracelets, and ask ourselves, What Would Jesus Do? In Mark 11/John 2, we see Jesus blow a gasket when some money-hungry bigots pull some shady shenanigans preventing people from worshiping. They were charging astronomical prices for the sacrificial animals required to forgive their sins. It wasn't the fact they were selling trinkets in church. This was the only section of the temple that Gentiles would be allowed in, so the money-changers' greediness essentially separated an entire group of people away from God. He busts up in there with a whip and asks them "Is it not written, 'My house shall be called a house of prayer for all the nations'? But you have made it a den of robbers." Did you catch that? He said *all the nations*. Even though I'm His favorite, He loves all of y'all too. Every single person. We are all His favorite. If you want to see God, go gangster, try separating Him from His children like these fools did. Or like we do when we insist that our way of worshiping is the only path to God.

It breaks my heart to hear people say that they love Christ but not the Church because of their history of getting burnt. It is like telling your best friend that they are cool, but you hate their spouse. That animosity is going to affect your relationship with your friend. Pastor Peter Haas of Substance church is a hilarious author who wrote the book: *Pharisectomy: How to Joyfully Remove Your Inner Pharisee and Other Religiously Transmitted Diseases.*[3] He states, "The church is not a perfect place. And quite often Christians do a terrible job at reflecting His true nature. Perhaps now you'll understand that our heavenly Father has His arms open wide- not because you have done all of the right things, but because He has compassion on all He has made. And once we understand that it's not about us but Him living through us, there simply isn't anything left that can become diseased. Why? Because "you died, and your life is now hidden with Christ in God" (Col. 3:3)."

That's what it boils down to in a nutshell. We are called to die to ourselves and our religiously transmitted diseases daily and instead be carriers of Christ. Christianity isn't a message but a lifestyle. Our lives should be so joyful and Spirit-filled that it's contagious to those around us. It leaves a sour taste in the mouths of nonbelievers when we are filled with bigotry and judgmental attitudes. It makes our God look powerless to control us, much less the universe. He seems unloving and unfair. God isn't fair, but we receive the goodness of that unfairness via grace when we decide to surrender our lives over to His care. I can't call Rabbi Jesus my Lord and not do what He says (Luke 6:46). I have to remind myself daily that this isn't a T+ G/42 situation. I can't manipulate my way closer to Christ, nor can I have a savior complex and manipulate God into saving anyone else. Sure, I can pray for these things. But He's the boss, and doesn't fit into the boxes I try to shove Him into. Deep down inside I know I wouldn't want a God that I could manipulate. If I could pack Him up and shove Him in my pocket only to pull out when I need something, it wouldn't allow room for Him to come do supernatural miracles. I can only try my best to surrender, let Him remove the bad from my heart so he can fill it with a contagious joy that piques others curiosity about who the real Christ is.

Pharisaical Pirates

The movie *Groundhog Day*[4] was so impactful on popular culture that the term became part of the English lexicon to mean a monotonous, repetitive, and unpleasant situation. Actor Bill Murray plays a character named Phil who is trapped in a time loop that only he is aware of, forcing him to relive February 2nd (aka Groundhog Day) repeatedly. Realizing there are no consequences for his actions since he will continue to relive the same day, his behavior spirals out of control, much to our amusement. He tries to manipulate a woman named Rita into falling in love with him. Nothing goes as he plans it, so he eventually decides to use this curse for the greater good by helping others. In the end, he learns the key to life isn't what happens but how you react to it.

Life often feels like my own unique version of *Groundhog Day*. More often than I would like to admit I wake up feeling bleak and hopeless, forced to figure out how to cope with what feels like the same problems as yesterday. I speculate this is one of the reasons the thought of suicide has crept up in my mind so often. On my worst days, my brain gets stuck in a repetitive loop fantasizing about self-sabotage instead of faithfully trusting that God has everything handled. It's slowly getting better the closer I get to Christ, but I still have bad days. One of my favorite quotes misattributed to C.S. Lewis is "Isn't it funny how day by day nothing changes but when you look back everything is different."[5] Compared to where I was three years ago, everything is different. I don't know how I lived without Christ for so long. Like Phil, it wasn't until I changed my perspective that my actions changed, forever altering the course of my destiny for the better. The mind is more powerful than we realize.

Scientists have been trying to understand the full potential of the human mind for years and have only scratched the surface. It's comparable to an iceberg where only the surface is observable, yet the majority of it is submerged in the depths of the subconscious. Collectively, we seem to be individual icebergs all connected by the same vast ocean. No matter how different we are, we have the same desire deep within for supernatural mythology. Elie Wiesel once said "God made man because He loves stories."[6] It would appear from the variety of stories worldwide that our author God loaned us His pen to enjoy writing our own creations. Tales of sacrifice and heroism stir up within us a sense of longing. They are splintered fragments of a much more incredible story taking place, one that we subconsciously know that we should know.

Myths reflect the universal concerns of humanity throughout history: the origin of man, birth, death, the afterlife, and everything in between. They tap into something subconscious in all of us, putting humankind's collective wisdom into shared tales. At ages nine and eleven, my sons are at the golden apex of childhood, where they have complex imaginations that are fascinated with stories. They aren't in a Groundhog Day mentality like many adults are, and every day is fertile with the possibility of a new adventure. Their imaginations have taken them from dodging dinosaurs in prehistoric caves to endless pursuits for Pokémon. Some of my favorite scenarios of theirs have centered around pirates. Aye, aye, me lads aren't the only ones whose hearts have been stolen by freebooters looking for loot. Pirates have captured imaginations for centuries with tales of excitement, danger, and romance.

Thumbing their nose at traditional social conventions, they dress flamboyantly, live fast, and die young. They live by different moral codes and watch out for their own. We have similar fascinations with gangs, outlaws, and other tribes. We glamorize outlaws like Bonnie and my third cousin twice removed Clyde Barrow. In case you didn't know, being a gangster runs in my family. Until his dying breath, he longed for something more significant. There is a deep, often unspoken void in the human soul that feels all alone.

We want to find others that we can share life with who will make us feel accepted. The Pharisees weren't any different. They banded together like dangerous pirates and fought anyone that wasn't in their elite click. They watched out for their own and destroyed anyone in their way, even the Son of God.

What is the real root of the issue here? Whether pirate or Pharisee, these groups offer promises of coping with the world's pressures by herd mentality. It starts when people see others solving problems they have, so they mimic their character traits hoping their problems will also go away. Promises of safety, love, and companionship are attractive to anyone struggling with fear, feelings of uselessness, anger, frustration, resentment, or self-pity. We all want to feel less alone and for the world to seem less scary. However, membership comes at a price. The organization and its rules demand to be put on a pedestal by becoming number one in a person's life. It is a subtle form of idolatry and is a toxic mentality. The price of membership is disregarding God's command to place Himself first in our lives. This is prideful. Pride always comes before the fall. Ask satan. Remember, "Whoever exalts himself will be humbled, and whoever humbles himself will be exalted." (Matthew 23:12) This form of pride doesn't always come from a narcissistic place, but sometimes out of desperation when the odds are stacked against an individual merely trying to survive.

Whereas other people offer promises of coping with the world, God teaches us how to convert pressure instead of enduring it. Many spectacular things are formed under pressure, like diamonds and saints. Nearly every time God wanted to see someone do great things in Scripture, He allowed them to be put under pressure. Just take a stroll down the hall of greats in Hebrews 11 if you are ever feeling alone in carrying huge burdens. All of these men and women put their ultimate faith in God, and through tension, He created spiritual giants out of all these heroes. Not because they did everything perfectly. Lord knows most of them made huge blunders. But because they knew where their help came from and walked humbly with Him.

Rabbi Jesus

As a Gentile Christian, my motives for wanting to learn more about the Jewish culture have been seriously questioned. I've been wrongly accused of leaving the faith out of sheer ignorance. I don't take it offensively. As humans, we try to put everything in neat categories to make sense of the world. However, to grow, one needs to think outside the box. I like to look at it like this: if I have been called into an intimate relationship with Christ, I should probably know more about His background. He knows every hair on my head. I should want to know more about who He is as a person. I would be a horrible friend to Him if I only came to Him when I wanted something.

Christians oftentimes get so hyper-focused on Jesus being our Savior that we forget that He was primarily seen as a teacher by those closest to Him. The disciples refer to Jesus as "Rabbi" on more than one occasion. (John 1:38, Mark 9:5) The word *Rabbi* literally means "my master", and in Jesus' day it was a term of respect for a teacher of Scripture. It didn't become a formal title until after His death. The rabbis of Jesus's time traveled from village to village, teaching Scripture and telling parables. They weren't paid for their work and had to be invited to teach. In Spangler and Tverberg's extraordinary work *Sitting at The Feet of Rabbi Jesus,*[7] they point out that "First, Jesus must have been quite learned by the standards of his time. If not, he would never have been invited to teach. Even his toughest critics never questioned his scholarship. Second, Jesus must have been observant of the Torah. If he hadn't been, he would have been barred from even attending the synagogue, let alone speaking at it."

Everywhere Jesus went, He drew crowds wanting to hear Him teach. God came to earth, put on a flesh suit, and instead of sitting on a throne demanding worship, He chose to teach and humbly serve. We should be taking notes here and studying His way of life. He didn't come here to chastise and punish. However, He did call people out on their nonsense. In Matthew 23, Jesus calls the scribes and the Pharisees out in the form of seven woes, which paraphrased are:[8]

1. They taught about God but did not love God, which kept people out of heaven.

2. They converted people to a dead works-based religion.

3. They taught that an oath sworn by the temple was not binding, yet said that if sworn by the gold ornaments/sacrificial gifts, then it was binding.

4. Taught the law but did not practice the most important parts like justice, mercy, and faithfulness to God.

5. Presented a clean appearance but were actually dirty inside with hidden worldly desires like greed and self-indulgence.

6. They acted like they were righteous but were full of wickedness.

7. Professed love for the dead prophets of old and claimed they would never murder them, but in actuality, they had the same murderous desires running through their veins.

Rather than rejecting the religious people of His day, Jesus always turned their love of scriptures around to teach them more about who He was. God is the Word. (John 1:1) The scribes/Pharisees claim to love Scripture without loving Christ was a dead religion because the two are one and the same.

Unfortunately, more often than I would like to admit, there's the inner Pharisee in me that wants to walk around pointing the finger at everyone else and call them a Pharisee too. I went from previously behaving like the first prodigal son in Luke 15:11-32 to striving like the older Pharisee prodigal son to earn my love. Jesus showed us through his lifestyle that the goal is to become more like the Father. Remember, every Christian is to become a little Christ. When we turn our hearts over to Rabbi Jesus, our Master will show us how. This is why reading the word is so important. We see in Romans 10 that faith comes from hearing and hearing through the word of Christ. He isn't dead, but he is alive in us and with us. We spend time learning scripture, so that the Word is near us, in our mouths and our hearts. We learn that if we confess with our mouths and believe with our hearts, we will be saved, not because of our own goodness but because He is good. Although faith without works is dead, (James 2:17) our assignments for God should be done with a grateful heart instead of self-righteousness. When we accept our own identities as messy, imperfect Kingdom kids, we can love ourselves and others with agape love. Our daily lives will become messy like glitter confetti love bombs instead of blood-splattered crime scenes showing the evidence of where we stabbed others with the sword of the Spirit. (Hebrews 4:12) Let's stop stabbing people. The world has enough Pharisaical pirates.

There's A Hole In the Bucket Dear Yeshua

He's everything you want
He's everything you need
He's everything inside of you
That you wish you could be
He says all the right things
At exactly the right time
But he means nothing to you
And you don't know why
-Vertical Horizon

When my boys were in utero, I used to sing *Simple Man* by Lynyrd Skynyrd at the top of my lungs, hoping they would internalize the song's lyrics into their personalities before birth. That's where I was at the time, don't judge me. My mother used to play Mama Cass's version of *Dream a Little Dream of Me* to me as a small child. I often had the melody stuck in my head throughout my childhood, but for the life of me could not remember the lyrics. It wasn't until we moved to Minnesota when I was fifteen and found the cassette tape in the boxes that I rediscovered the origin of the melody that had calmed me to sleep many sleepless nights. My heart remembered what my mind could not. Maybe my boys will end up a simple kind of man when it is all is said and done because of the lyrics sung over them.

As the overall theme in this book, we've discussed how we are a product of our interactions with the world even prior to our conception. These are what made our stories, and *our* stories are important because we are all interconnected. It's honestly a wonder any of us are normal with the wide variety of disturbing fairy tales/nursery rhymes in the world as our first role models. I was especially disappointed as an adult with my childhood favorite, *Beauty and the Beast*, with its glorification of Stockholm Syndrome. I banned the movie from my house. Although if I had to pick a Disney princess, I would still choose Belle because of her gigantic library. I'd just shoot the beast and stick his head on my wall decorated with a tiara.

For real though, what are we teaching our children? My Dad always said you could convince children that anything is a great idea if you have the right vocal inflection. To further prove his point, he would sweetly ask us if we wanted to have live child sacrifices in the same way you would ask a child if they wanted to go get ice cream. Did I mention I get my dark sense of humor from my father? But he has a valid point. With enough razzle-dazzle, you can make any story sound enchanting. With generations of children being soothed to sleep with The Brothers Grimm fairy tales, it's no wonder we ended up with a society full of deranged sociopaths. It's vital to be intentional about what we feed our souls. These stories become interwoven into the fabric of our existence, and we begin to normalize things that are appalling.

It isn't all bad though. We get some beneficial life lessons from fairy tales. We learn the value of hope, hard work and helping one another. However, I am still waiting on delightful singing creatures to come to clean my house. Looking at you, Disney. That was a cruel false representation of reality. So was the false notion that the world is a musical and that it is perfectly acceptable to burst out into contagious song/dance no matter what the occasion might be. I still see nothing wrong with this, so if you hate musicals, you might want to steer clear of my vicinity.

Speaking of catchy songs, one childhood nursery rhyme that I often find stuck in my head is called *There's a Hole in the Bucket*.[1] In case you aren't familiar, it's a circular back and forth conversation between two people named Liza and Henry about how to fix a hole in their bucket. A variety of outlandish solutions to repair it are presented (such as plugging it with straw), which eventually circles back to needing to draw water with the bucket to fix the tools needed for the restorations. Yet, the bucket still has a hole in it, and the song loop starts all over again. Teach your children this tune and Lamb Chop's *The Song That Never Ends*, and you will have given them the tools to turn all of your hair gray in no time.

Have you ever tried to carry water in a bucket with a hole in it? If so, you probably lost more water than you could carry. It's not very productive. Yet many of us carry on with our spiritual lives in this way. Most of us haven't let Jehovah Rapha in to repair the damage to all areas of our hearts, so our hearts are analogous to leaky buckets. We hold on to our perceived control, and we try to cope with the wounds. We walk around trying to draw living water from everyone around us when all they have to offer is unwholesome water held in their impaired hearts. It's exhausting. Only Jesus can give the gift of eternal living water. (John 4:13-14) Even a good person makes a bad Jesus. Resentment and disappointment towards others are often indicators you have been trying to draw living water from the wrong cistern. Cisterns aren't always people. They are whatever we are putting our faith in. This tendency has been going on for generations. El Quanna had to call the Israelites out in Jeremiah 2:13, "For my people have committed two evils: they have forsaken me, the fountain of living waters, and hewed out cisterns for themselves, broken cisterns that can hold no water." They had a nasty habit of idolatry. So do we. As the old cliche says, those who don't learn history are doomed to repeat it.

This is why it is so important to examine our life stories thoroughly. Inspection of my life saga has shown that I've tried to draw pungent water from various faulty wells, varying from my quest to Boaz to my numerous addictions. Shoot, even my obsessive striving toward perfection is grasping at straws instead of Yeshua. The saying "grasping at straws" is a metaphor alluding to the observation that a drowning person will desperately attempt to grasp at anything to escape their predicament. Straw isn't typically a good solution, as our friends Liza and Henry above discovered when trying to repair the hole in their bucket with straw instead of something more practical. Only when I allowed Jesus to come into my heart and repair the holes from the inside out did I begin to notice any changes in my sanity. Coping with pain instead of letting Christ convert it is like doing the same thing over and over again and expecting different results, aka insanity. This mending work never ceases. It isn't a one-and-done process. It's easier to carry water to my neighbors now that I'm less dehydrated. The more I interact with people, the more scar tissue (that I wish you saw) my bucket will incur because hurt people hurt people. Even after He gave me a more functional heart, I still have to spend time with Him daily, asking Him to fill it back up with His living water.

Take Down the High Places

One of the most vital parts of spending time daily with Adonai is reading my Bible. I'm out of my mind excited that my dad is reading it for the first time. It's like a gift from both of my fathers, my earthly one and my heavenly One, because I want to spend eternity with both of them forever. Dad is taking steps to meet me where I'm at because he loves me and knows how much I love Jesus. I'm taking steps to be less of a Pharisee towards him and trying to love him more unconditionally. El Roi loves us both dearly and is faithful in taking steps to draw us both back to Him. He hears my prayers. Dad's in either 1st or 2nd Chronicles at the time I'm writing this, and he made me smile the other day when he asked if it was going to get any better. I can remember being there myself the first time I read through the Word, and even now, some sections can seem monotonous and irrelevant. In actuality, it's all relevant, so I should say it seems irrelevant to me at the time instead. Almost every time I read through it, if I dig a little deeper, I can usually pick up a new little gem to store in my heart to pull out later. The same passages can seem different from the last time I read them. They call the Bible the *Living Word* because the Holy Spirit will give you new revelation each time you read it.

I think it was my second or third run through the Bible when I noticed somewhere in Kings that they kept referring over and over again to these things called "high places." Over and over and over again, God is giving a report card of how each of the kings performed during their reign, and their decision to remove the high places was being used as a metric to determine how well they pleased God. But why on El Elyon's green earth does this matter? Because it shows what they let take priority in their heart. These "high places" were places of pagan worship, most often built on high hills or mountains and under trees to bring people closer to false Gods. The worship would include sacrifices, burning incense, and rituals. They were commanded to destroy all of these places.

The Israelites were God's chosen people to be set apart to be holy, (Leviticus 20:26) and as Gentiles, we have been grafted into the family tree. The definition of holy is set apart, dedicated, or consecrated to God. When we strive for holiness in our lives, we aren't striving for perfection. Instead, we aspire to be set apart from the world for God's intended use in our lives. He warned them that their blessings would be turned into curses unless they took steps to prevent the worship of false idols. Peyton Jones in the *Through the Word*[2] app talks about the high places in 2 Kings 15's lesson. He uses the metaphor comparing the heart to a "traitor gate," which was a hidden door in a castle initially designed for royalty to have an escape route in times of trouble. Sometimes an enemy with the desire to destroy the king would successfully bribe a king's servant to gain illegal access into the castle. We are also being bribed this way as Christians, and the enemy wants to kill our King, El Shaddai, by gaining access into our hearts.

We are instructed to give no opportunities to the devil (Ephesians 4:27) and advised not to let the world in the traitor gate either. (Colossians 2:8-10) This is why God wanted the Israelites to remove the high places in their surroundings and why we must do so in our lives. They are traitor gates that will lead us down paths of destruction and away from God by worshiping false idols. The high places have to be exposed before they can be eradicated. Once they are exposed, we must sacrifice the natural to make room for the Spiritual so we don't forsake our hope of steadfast love for vain idols. (Jonah 2:8) We are told in 2 Corinthians 5:16-17, "From now on, therefore, we regard no one according to the flesh. Even though we once regarded Christ according to the flesh, we regard him thus no longer. Therefore, if anyone is in Christ, he is a new creation. The old has passed away; behold the new has come."

The definition of worship is to show reverence and adoration for something. God is always worshiping. We see that with the Son giving glory to the Father, the Spirit leading us all back to Him with reverence. Since we are made in the image of God, we are created for worship. What high places are you worshiping that aren't God? Are they sex, drugs and rock and roll? What about power, wealth or fame? Celebrities or politics? Your personal paradigm of righteousness? Are your traitor gates your love for astrology or horoscopes? Tarot cards or crystal cleansing? We laugh at the Israelites' ignorance in Exodus 32 when they built a golden calf to worship. They were saved, rescued from Egypt, shown God's grace continually through miracles despite their grumbling, and they still didn't believe Jehovah Jireh would provide. But really, how different are we from them? When we believe the promises of the enemy or the golden lies of the world, we cheat God of the only thing he requires of us: our adoration. He doesn't want our works. All He wants is our love, respect and obedience.

What does Moses do when he comes down from the mountain to this horrific sight? He takes the golden calf, grinds it down, scatters it on water, and makes the people drink it. (Exodus 32:20) When I came across this on my third run-through of the Bible, my spiritual Spidey senses went off, and I went into sleuth mode to figure out why Moses would make them drink it. I came to the conclusion that anything we eat is subject to the normal process of human digestion. So eventually, the things we eat will be discarded as waste. In essence, Moses made them drink the golden calf to learn that their false idols were crap. Let this lesson in excrement be a reminder to us to thank Jehovah Raah for our blessings, as we let Him guide us back home and away from the high places the world offers.

Say My Name, Say My Name

I don't know if you have been picking up what I've been throwing down this chapter, but I have used a variety of God's names throughout this section. Like a precious diamond, our God is also multifaceted, and His variety of names show different sides of His personality. Sometimes we need Him as Yeshua, our savior who rescues us. Other times as Jehovah Rapha, the God who heals. Moses and the Israelites saw Him as El Quanna, our jealous God. One day every knee will bow to Adonai, our Lord and master. Sometimes we need El Roi, the strong one who sees, who is also El Elyon, our most high God. El Shaddai, Lord God almighty, shows himself as Jehovah Jireh, who provides all we need. No matter how he reveals

Himself, I trust Jehovah Raah as my shepherd who will guide me through it all.[3]

Although it might appear as though God has multiple personality disorder, He is showing us his nature and character through his various names. The Bible is meant to reveal who God is, and show us what He is like by teaching us what He has done throughout history. The birth of the Messiah is predicted many times throughout the Old Testament. Isaiah 9:6-7 in particular tells us, "For to us a child is born, to us a son is given; and the government shall be upon his shoulder, and his name shall be called Wonderful Counselor, Mighty God, Everlasting Father, Prince of Peace. Of the increase of his government and of peace there will be no end, on the throne of David and over his Kingdom, to establish it and to uphold it with justice and with righteousness from this time forth and forevermore. The zeal of the Lord of hosts will do this." No wonder people were confused when Jesus arrived on the scene. The Jews were expecting a military leader, not the sacrificial Lamb of God. To this day they have a veil over their hearts that cannot see God's promises to their people delivered through Yeshua. (2 Corinthians 3:14-15)

Although it may not look like it by the state of things, the King of Kings has everything under control. The world is dangerously deceptive and hostile towards God. Though satan's forces still rage, we are empowered by the same Holy Spirit that empowered Christ so that we can stand firm. The day is coming when the loyalty of God's true followers will be revealed and their suffering will be rewarded. Only those who proclaim the name of Christ as their Lamb of God, who came to bear their sins on His shoulders will live in eternity with Him. We are asked to fear pain less, and desire humility more as we bow down and worship Jesus Christ our Lord above anything the enemy/world offers.

We live in a society that often says "God" instead of saying Jesus. I catch myself doing this intentionally sometimes, especially if I'm surrounded by non-believers. Or if I know someone has severe church wounds. I always beat myself up about it later and am filled with shame that I didn't proclaim the name of Christ when I should have. I can almost hear Jesus singing Destiny's Child's song *Say My Name*, telling me to stop acting shady and asking why the sudden change. He knows my heart in that most of the time this comes from a fearful place that isn't trying to deny him. Instead, I want to draw others closer to Him by my actions rather than my words, and I know the name of Jesus scares people who have been stabbed by Pharisees. Yet sin is still sin, which misses the mark. If I listen hard enough, I can hear the rooster crow like Peter. I'm slowly learning to turn this over, surrendering my shame and asking the Holy Spirit to fill me with more courage in the future. It's all about progress not perfection.

He Knows You by Name

I might fail to say His name at times, but He never fails to say mine. Even in my shortcomings, I am reminded in Isaiah 43 not to "fear because the Lord has redeemed me and called me by name because I am His. I perceive He is doing a new thing in my life, and it is springing up from within the fountain of my heart." There are still holes in my bucket, but day by day, He restores me. The more whole my heart becomes, the holier I will act because the two go hand in hand. Don't get me wrong. I'm still stubborn and hard-headed. Even so, at least I am no longer running away from God's will for my life like Jonah because I know Jesus loves me. When I quiet my heart long enough to concentrate on the whisper, I can hear Him tell me so.

On December 6th of 2020, Max Lucado came to speak at Community Bible Church as a guest speaker with a message titled Peace on Earth: Perhaps Today. I was having a particularly rough time that week. With Christmas rapidly approaching, my finances were drained as well as my spirit. Twenty-four minutes into the service, Pastor Ed asked anyone struggling financially to step out into the aisle. I was too scared to step out in faith, and my heart immediately regretted choosing fear when they handed everyone in the aisle bags with $100. Touched by their need, the people surrounding these brave souls started handing them whatever they had in their pockets to further help out. This is one of the things I love most about my church.

They put their money where their mouth is. If they see a need, they fill a need.

However, this was the straw that broke the camel's back on this particular day, I lost it. Once the service commenced, I began bawling. My heart just couldn't take anymore. To make matters worse, this mini meltdown took place with a mask on due to the pandemic. It was like the flood gates had opened, and there was no stopping the tears even if people were looking. After a little while, I finally regained some composure. That's when Johnna's developmentally disabled uncle looked straight at me and said, "Wow, I felt like I needed to cry too but not *THAT* much!". Sometimes I believe that man is truly an angel in disguise. I turned my attention over to Max Lucado, but by the time he started talking, a bitter root towards God had already sprouted in my heart. I know I was being a spoiled brat here, but for whatever reason, this incident triggered all of the false insecurities I've carried over the years that God doesn't care about me. I can relate to Jonah sitting in the shade under the plant God had provided, stewing in his sour feelings because the universe wasn't being run like he thought it should. Any rate, the longer I listened to Max, the angrier I got with God.

I started venting to him in my head, letting Him know that it seemed like He had utterly forgotten me. Mind you, minutes prior, He had just given me an opportunity to get financial help, but I was too chicken to step out and ask for it. This is why it is so important to stop and take inventory of feelings versus facts. Any rate, I clearly wasn't in the right headspace that day, so that helpful exercise never came to mind. As I'm fuming, I start bargaining with God by asking for a sign like Gideon's fleece. My internal dialogue looked something like this, "God, I've had about enough of this and I can't take any more. I think you are a jerk, and I really don't want anything to do with you from this point on. You see me struggling down here, and yet you leave me broken. Why on earth would you pull me out of the fire just to watch me drown? I hear all these incredible stories about you performing miracles where you randomly have people give messages from you to other strangers all the time. If you are still here with me, I want you to have Max Lucado say my name right now, out loud, on stage. If not, then shove it." In all honesty, it was probably worse but I'm really trying my best not to swear as much.

Ashamedly, I was pretty close to throwing my hands up that day and going back to my former lifestyle without Christ. I sat there listening intently to hear if Max was actually going to say my name out loud. Around an hour and three minutes into this ordeal (I've looked it up to make sure I'm not crazy), he starts telling this story about Qantas airlines selling tickets for "The Flight to Nowhere" in Australia. People missed flying so much during the pandemic that the tickets were completely sold out in less than ten minutes. As he was telling the story, he showed a picture of the flight path on the screen to reiterate that. It was indeed a circle that led to nowhere. There were a bunch of what looked like airport codes, none of which were words, and right there in the top middle, as clear as day, there was the name TASHA. I was immediately awestruck. I look over at Johnna to ask her if she is seeing what I'm seeing, but before I can get a word out, she says "Yes, I see it, Tasha. He must really love you."

Just in case you were skeptical, here it is:

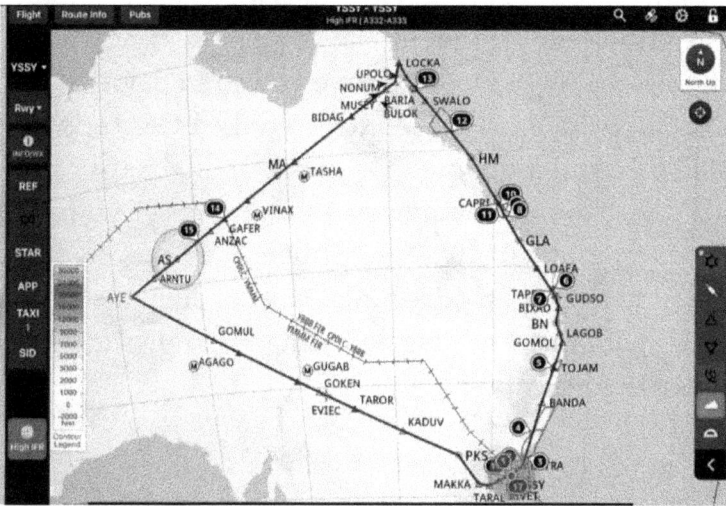

Of course, my name never came out of Mr. Lucado's mouth like I asked for. I like to think of it as God's subtle way of telling me that He is on the throne and I'm not. He knew how bad I needed Him at that moment. I needed to see the Immanuel, God with us, side of His personality. Throughout the Bible, He bends over backward to show His people that He is always there with them. In the wilderness, He leads them with a cloud by day and a fire by night. He sends signs and prophets and even sent His son. Our sinful nature seems to be firmly embedded in our DNA, and humanity never fails to put the wrong things first. We fall, yet when we turn our hearts to Him, He is always there waiting to pick us right back up.

Let the words of Jonah 2:7-10 be a reminder, "When my life was fainting away, I remembered the LORD, and my prayer came to you, into your holy temple. Those who pay regard to vain idols forsake their hope of steadfast love. But I with the voice of thanksgiving will sacrifice to you; what I have vowed to pay. Salvation belongs to the LORD! And the LORD spoke to the fish, and it vomited Jonah out upon the dry land." May my testimony never involve being vomited up by a fish. May I always remember the Lord is with me and to not ingest false idols. Most of all, may I come to Him with thanksgiving, knowing He knows my name and loves me so.

דברי הימים

Chronicles

*"We're all stories in the end.
Just make it a good one eh?"*
-The Doctor

The Tanakh (sometimes called the Hebrew Bible) ends with the book of Chronicles, or Divrê Hayyāmîm in Hebrew, which is translated as "the words of the days."[1] It isn't clear when Christians reorganized the canon and split Chronicles in two. Malachi, originally found right before Psalms, was most likely chosen as the end of the Christian canon because it served as a fitting bridge between the Old Testament and the New Testament. The prophet points out the hearts of the people were not changed even after generations in Babylonian captivity. They were in desperate need of a savior. It ends with a curse, "Behold, I will send you Elijah the prophet before the great and awesome day of the LORD comes. And he will turn the hearts of the fathers to their children and the hearts of the children to their fathers, lest I come and strike the land with a decree of utter destruction." Malachi 4:5-6. I bet Malachi didn't get invited to too many dinner parties either. I couldn't handle his calling.

On the other hand, Chronicles serves as a genealogy of Jesus. It ends with Cyrus, the king of Persia, declaring, "The LORD, the God of heaven, has given me all the kingdoms of the earth, and he has charged me to build him a house at Jerusalem, which is in Judah. Whoever is among you of all his people, may the LORD his God be with him. Let him go up." That last sentence may appear complete in English, but in Hebrew it is incomplete. Therefore, if you find any incomplete sentences in this book, I can therefore argue it is biblically acceptable if it gets the point across. All joking aside, the Bible Project's article *The Sense of an Ending: What is the real last book of the Old Testament?*[2] argues that the purpose of this incomplete sentence was to remind us that the promise to David had not been fulfilled at the time of the Israelites return from exile. It serves as a hyperlink that points to Daniel 9, making the connection that Israel still had another round of exile ahead of them before the real Kingdom of God would come. How that all works is beyond my paygrade, so I will let the scholars hash out the details about how many years that is.

In my opinion, the ending of Chronicles seems more in line with the purpose of Jesus rather than the curse that the book of Malachi offers. However, I'm sure God in His sovereignty allowed the reorganization for a reason. Although the Messiah has already come, we are anxiously awaiting His return to establish the Kingdom of God on earth. Until that day comes, we have a piece of Him in the scriptures since He was the Word in the flesh. (John 1:1) Need I remind you of the power of words? You might not need the reminder, but I sure do because I am prone to forget. Genesis doesn't say he made the universe with His hands. It says God *spoke* the universe into existence. Since we are made in His image, our words are also that powerful. We speak things into existence every day. Word by word, sentence by sentence. This is how all stories are written. Which brings the meaning of this book full circle. How are you writing *your* chronicles?

During our time together, we've discussed some rather difficult things. Examining our stories in the open often brings any buried negative emotions to the surface. That is perfectly normal, and is part of the process. Tension is vital for any story. It's what grips the reader and keeps them coming back for more. So don't view the tension in your life as an insurmountable obstacle or something to avoid. Make the conscientious choice to view stress as the stakes that make us committed to the development of our character. Without stakes, there is no story because the reader isn't as emotionally invested. Our stories were designed to contain adventure, plot twists, mystery, suspense, controversy, protagonists/antagonists, backstories, and cliff hangers. These elements give our lives a rich complexity and an engaging plot, so we can engage with others and share our narrative with the world. The world needs to hear what you have to say, and no one else can say it like you. You are building a legacy. Make sure you are building it on a firm foundation.

Another Brick in The Wall

Almost every year, my dad comes to stay with the boys and I for the holidays. A few days ago, he convinced me to join him in watching *Roger Waters: The Wall*.[3] I don't spend much time watching movies anymore, but since I had hit my own metaphorical wall with this book, I figured it would be a good thing to spend some time with him and get out of my head. Although I grew up listening to their music, I didn't know very much about Pink Floyd. I have to say, I was very impressed. Roger and the group can captivate an audience like no other. The concert film takes his strong antiwar stance and interweaves it with his personal mission to see the memorial in Italy dedicated to his father he lost in the war as a small child. It's extremely moving and the visuals are breathtaking. What a powerful legacy.

Sitting there with my dad, I realize I'm more like him than I will ever know. It appears we have both sought throughout our lives to be understood and loved by a world that denied us what we crave most in the secret depths of our souls. We both caught fleeting glimpses, but agape love always seemed elusive and evasive. God showed me in that moment that my father has always tried to be there for me, and that it was I who had built up protective walls around my heart. I often fail to recognize the pain he has endured, and I've never given him enough credit. I've always demanded life on my terms, just as he often does. I'm grateful he's lost his temper and mellowed out in his older age, but worry that he's grown comfortably numb to the absence of Jesus in his life. On the other hand, I have become more high-strung in my neurotic tendencies. Both are coping mechanisms. Both are walls we have built to make sense of our existences.

We are both in our own worlds, having been burnt so many times that the thought of truly letting someone in (Jesus for him, the world for me) doesn't naturally resonate with our logic-loving minds. Yet succumbing to the isolation we lose a piece of ourselves. Emotions and logic are both integral to the human experience. Without love and logic, life has no meaning. Grace and Truth. We are all enrolled in the school of life. The curriculum is to learn to love Jesus and love ourselves and others like He did. To learn to walk humbly. That's pretty much it. When pain comes, it is a gift and we thank God for it, asking Him how to use it. I have noticed in my short life that Christians seem to handle pain better. It isn't because they are wiser or stronger. It is because they don't have to handle it alone. We have a Father to hold our hands. While I'm tremendously blessed to have an earthly father who has held my hand throughout the years, I have expected the same level of perfection from him that embodies our heavenly Father. This isn't fair to him and it screws up my relationship with both fathers, isolating me from both.

Fear adds another brick in the wall. The walls we build around our hearts often don't keep out the bad as much as they prevent the good from getting in. When we have Christ, we have it all. Not from the world's perspective and not a problem-free life. We are given a true inner peace that is unexplainable. He stands at the door or our hearts knocking, (Revelation 3:20) but we can't hear him if we have a wall built around our hearts. I know it's not a popular message, but one day we will stand trial before Him. (Romans 14:10) As believers, we have nothing to worry about, as He has removed our sins as far as the east is from the west. (Psalm 103:12) I pray daily for the Holy Spirit to speak to the nonbelievers in my life, including my dad. I can't imagine him not being there holding my hand for the best concert of all time as we worship the King of Kings for eternity.

The climactic song The Trial by Pink Floyd concludes both the album and the original film. The lyrics pierce my heart, "Since, my friend, you have revealed your deepest fear- I sentence you to be exposed before your peers- Tear down the wall." The trials I have experienced have torn down my walls, and continue to do so. They have taught me that I'm stronger than I think I am, and I have little to fear with God on my side. When I remember to surrender to His will, He has always directed me where I need to be. At times I still fear the outcome, afraid God doesn't want the same things I want for my life. I've heard the acronym for fear is: False Expectations Appearing Real. Stacking enough bricks of fear together leads to a life isolated from God. Pausing to pray during these moments reminds me He is never more than a thought or breath away. We are eternally connected.

The Weird Science of Abiding

We've covered a lot of ground, and the path hasn't been linear. Kudos to you! You are stronger than you think you are too. I couldn't end our time together without being weird and revisiting the concept of cellular memory. Considered to be pseudoscience by some, it does bring up an interesting theory on how the transfer of memories might lie within our cells. There have been too many stories of heart transplant recipients acquiring the personality traits of their donors to not quietly ask ourselves if there is a phenomenon going on there that science can't explain yet.[4] For example, it's common to hear stories of the recipients suddenly developing cravings for food that they never liked before, only to find out that their donor loved these foods. There have been true accounts of people remembering things that have never happened to them. The craziest one I have heard to date is when a man received a heart from a suicide victim, only to leave his wife for the donor's wife, eventually ending with him becoming depressed and committing suicide in the same exact manner.

Maybe the ancient world wasn't so crazy after all. Maybe the heart *is* the physical/intellectual/emotional moral center of life. This theory of cellular memory would explain why even after thousands of years we still hold on to the original sin nature of Adam and Eve in the garden. Maybe we have more in common with amoebas than we know. This would explain why our hearts beg us to do things we know we don't want to do. It would also explain why we long for a home we have never been to. Our hearts know in faith things our finite minds can't possibly comprehend. Our cellular memory knows the truth of our collective history and reminds our hearts that they were designed to walk humbly in the garden with God. I am not a scientist, so I can't prove or disprove this theory. All I can do is live in the present and abide in the Vine.

John 15:1-11 uses the word "abide" ten times. When a word is used ten times within eleven verses, it stands to reason the speaker is going above and beyond to draw emphasis to that particular word: *abide*. According to *Strong's Concordance*[5] the original word for abide is "menó," which means to stay, remain, or wait. Within the context of this verse, He wants to be connected to us as closely as a branch is connected to a vine. It implies oneness between two things. Jesus is Immanuel, God with us, and He wants to abide in the home in our heart.

The word abide paints the picture of living in a home or living in fellowship with those we love. Jesus was always being invited to people's houses. The Holy Spirit was given to the Jews on Pentecost in Acts 2 in a home, and He was given to the Gentiles in Acts 10 in Cornelius' home. The worship of God should be central to our homes as we raise our families as Christians. This is why our homes are attacked by the enemy so hard. This is why our childhood homes were often successfully attacked, sometimes severed from the Vine. Satan knows if he can knock us out coming out of the gate, we will begin to identify with the ways of the world. The customs of Babylon will feel normal, and we will worship false gods. He will do whatever it takes in an attempt to detour Kingdom kids from reproducing more Kingdom kids.

I ask God on a daily basis to protect my household and invite Him to abide with us. The boys and I pray, study scripture, and read devotionals together to fill our hearts with His Word. They need these weapons because they are like Daniel in the lion's den, and they need to know the God of Israel as they go to school in Babylon. In my daily prayers I ask God to break the generational curses that run on both sides of their family, and to fill them with the Holy Spirit so they will become warriors for Christ. As a single Mom, the enemy tries to plant doubts about my ability to be able to raise strong men without being a man. I recognize his lies, and know that if I can't teach them something He will send someone into their lives who can. My heart knows deep within that the answer to all anxiety is remembering that the outcomes for any situation belong with the one who designed it all. I am only responsible for my efforts. Nothing will be impossible with God. (Luke 1:37) John 15:7 tells us that if we abide in Him and His Word, then we can ask whatever we wish and it will be given to us. The tricky part is wrangling the heart into abiding.

The Choice Is Yours

"You take the blue pill, the story ends. You wake up in your bed and believe whatever you want to. You take the red pill, you stay in Wonderland, and I will show you how deep the rabbit hole goes. Remember, all I'm offering is the truth. Nothing more."
- Morpheus, The Matrix[6]

We might not be in the Matrix like Neo, but there is an unseen realm to this world that is more complex than we will ever know. You won't need to decide between two pills to alter the course of your eternal destiny, but you do have to choose whether you will have faith and swallow the truth. Will you accept the righteous red blood shed for you on the cross, and follow Jesus for eternity? No one can make that choice for you. This path might seem uncertain, but it holds the key to your freedom. Freedom from the enslaving control of the enemy's lies and the world. Like Neo found out, knowing the truth behind the illusion is a harsher and more difficult reality. The road is long, and the cross is heavy. However, it will forever change your perception of reality. I beg you, don't be a slave to this world. It might offer promises of comfort and peace, but ultimately, it's a prison designed to make you think you have to work hard to be loved. You think you can do these things but you just can't, Nemo! You don't have to work so hard. You are already loved.

No matter what you choose, there is no judgment from me. The purpose of this book wasn't to shove anything down your throat. It was just to set out the tasty platter of truth in front of you at the table so we can break bread together. "Taste and see that the LORD is good! Blessed is the man who takes refuge in him!" (Psalms 34:8) Take what you want from it, leave the rest behind. I encourage you to do your own research, and not take my words at face value. It's like a treasure hunt that never ends. There are lots of hidden truths to be uncovered. Be sure to write your discoveries down, because we are prone to forget, and it's helpful to be able to look back to find healing and happiness. Ponder them in your heart. Share them with others.

On this journey, there are plenty of twists and turns. If you fall into the pit on your adventures, it is only the end if you stay there. Pit happens and that's an unfortunate part of life. But get back up, dust yourself off and try again. We are going to make mistakes, and that's okay. Like kintsugi they can become the most beautiful parts about us. It isn't about the goal, but about the straining towards Jesus. "Not that I have already obtained this or am already perfect, but I press on to make it my own, because Christ Jesus has made me his own." (Philippians 3:12) Even in the moments we do everything perfectly, God will take little notice if we aren't loving. We never feel as close as we are to God as we do in our compassionate moments. That's the example Immanuel set for us to live out our lives. When we show selfless agape love with one another, that's how we know we have found God. We love because He first loved us. (1 John 4:19) God is love.

Even if this book has accomplished nothing else, I pray that I have at least sparked an interest within you to examine your own story. Within it, you will find the answers to the questions your heart has been asking all along. Your story contains God's healing, grace, and truth. It is unique to you, and no one else can examine it like you can. This requires getting out of autopilot and doing a spiritual EKG. What are you acting out that you haven't worked out? In what ways are you hiding in the baggage? What unforgiveness towards others are you poisoning yourself with? Do you know YOU are loved? What versions of the T + G/42 formula are you calculating in an attempt to manipulate God? Regardless of the answers, I pray you can be a jellyfish in a world full of sharks as you love the mirrors around you. Use your unwanted gifts to grow and heal instead of becoming a Pharisaical pirate. Look towards Rabbi Jesus as your example. He will expose the high places in your life and show you the way back to Himself, where true love and joy are found. None of us are perfect, but we're all doing our best.

שָׁלוֹם

Shalom

NOTES

Unless otherwise indicated, all Scripture quotations are from The ESV® Bible (The Holy Bible, English Standard Version®), copyright © 2001 by Crossway, a publishing ministry of Good News Publishers. Used by permission. All rights reserved."

Introduction

1.Adamson, Dave. *52 Hebrew Words Every Christian Should Know*, Christian Art Gifts, Vereeniging, 2018, pp. 42–43.
2.*Alcoholics Anonymous*, ALCOHOLICS ANONYMOUS SERVICES INC, New York, 2001, pp. 60–62.

א Chapter One- Spiritual EKG

Epigraph: "10 Nikola Tesla Quotes That Still Apply Today." *Lifehack*, Lifehack, 21 Sept. 2015, https://www.lifehack.org/305348/10-nikola-tesla-quotes-that-still-apply-today.
1. Goleman, Daniel. Social Intelligence: The New Science of Human Relationships, Bantam Books, New York, NY, 2007, p. 4.
2. Strong, James, and James Strong. *The New Strong's Expanded Exhaustive Concordance of the Bible*. Thomas Nelson, 2010.
3. *Twelve Steps and Twelve Traditions*, Alcoholics Anonymous World Services, New York, 1981, p. 42.
4. "9 Secrets to Leading Sheep - No Matter How Many Legs They Have." *RapidStart Leadership*, 21 July 2021, https://www.rapidstartleadership.com/leading-sheep/.
5. "What Is an Electrocardiogram (EKG or ECG) Test: Purpose & Types." *WebMD*, WebMD,

https://www.webmd.com/heart-disease/electrocardiogram-ekgs.

6. Lawrence, and Marshall Davis. *The Practice of the Presence of God in Modern English*. Marshall Davis, 2013.

7. Brown C. Brené. *The Gifts of Imperfection Let Go of Who You Think You're Supposed to Be and Embrace Who You Are*, Center City, Minn.: Hazelden Publishing, 2010, p. 6.

ב Chapter Two- Our Childhoods and How They Form Us

Epigraph: Vanzant, Iyanla. "How to Heal the Wounds of Your Past." *Oprah.com*, Oprah.com, 11 Oct. 2011, https://www.oprah.com/oprahs-lifeclass/iyanla-vanzant-how-to-heal-the-wounds-of-your-past.

1. Campbell, Mike. "Biblical Names." *Behind the Name - the Etymology and History of First Names*, https://www.behindthename.com/names/usage/biblical.

2. Adamson, Dave. *52 Hebrew Words Every Christian Should Know*, Christian Art Gifts, Vereeniging, 2018, p. 23.

3. Strong, James, and James Strong. *The New Strong's Expanded Exhaustive Concordance of the Bible*. Thomas Nelson, 2010.

4. Baker, Amy. *Picture Perfect: When Life Doesn't Line Up*, New Growth Press, Greensboro, NC, 2014, p. 55.

5. Israel, Ira. *How to Survive Your Childhood Now That You're an Adult: A Path to Authenticity and Awakening*, New World Library, Novato (California), 2017, Introduction.

6. Author Pamela Li, MS. "4 Types of Parenting Styles and Their Effects on the Child." *Parenting For Brain*, 27 Dec. 2021, https://www.parentingforbrain.com/4-baumrind-parenting-styles/.

7. Kimmel, Tim. *Grace-Based Parenting: Set Your Family Free*, W Pub. Group, Nashville, TN, 2005, p. 172.

‌ Chapter Three- Innocence Lost

Epigraph:"A Quote by James Garbarino." *Goodreads*, Goodreads, https://www.goodreads.com/quotes/1280088-the-initial-trauma-of-a-young-child-may-go-underground.

1. Cherry, Kendra. "How Does Repression Work in Our Unconscious Mind?" *Verywell Mind*, Verywell Mind, 25 Apr. 2021, https://www.verywellmind.com/repression-as-a-defense-mechanism-4586642#:~:text=Repression%20is%20the%20unconscious%20blocking,feelings%20of%20guilt%20and%20anxiety.

2. Esrick, Michelle, director. *Cracked Up: The Darrell Hammond Story*. 2019.

3. Hammond, Darrell. *God, If You're Not up There ...: Tales of Stand-up, Saturday Night Live, and Other Mind-Altering Mayhem*. Harper, 2012.

4. "Why Do Deer Get Transfixed by Car Headlights and Freeze in Place?" *Science ABC*, 12 Nov. 2021, https://www.scienceabc.com/nature/animals/why-do-deer-get-transfixed-by-car-headlights-and-freeze-in-place.html.

5. Selby, Jenn. "'Why Didn't She Fight Back?" the Myth That's Used to Justify Sexual Violence." *Why Freezing Up Is A Common Response During Rape*, https://www.refinery29.com/en-gb/2020/03/9547973/freezing-up-response-rape.

6. "Climatize Definition and Meaning: Collins English Dictionary." *Climatize Definition and Meaning | Collins English Dictionary*, HarperCollins Publishers Ltd, https://www.collinsdictionary.com/us/dictionary/english/climatize.

7. "Judith Lewis Herman Quotes." *Quotefancy*, https://quotefancy.com/quote/2264728/Judith-Lewis-Herman-Recovery-unfolds-in-three-stages-The-central-task-of-the-first-stage.

8. "National Sexual Assault Hotline." *RAINN*, https://www.rainn.org/.

9. Frankl, Viktor E. *Man's Search for Meaning*. Beacon Press, 2014.

⁊ Chapter Four- Fun Times Or Dirty Lies?

1. "List of Twelve-Step Groups." *Wikipedia*, Wikimedia Foundation, 6 Dec. 2021, https://en.wikipedia.org/wiki/List_of_twelve-step_groups.

2.*Twelve Steps and Twelve Traditions*, Alcoholics Anonymous World Services, New York, 1981, p. 76.

ה Chapter Five- The Dark Night Of The Soul

1. "Youversion Bible App." *YouVersion*, 4 Nov. 2021, https://www.youversion.com/the-bible-app/.

2. 30, Lawrence S. CunninghamJanuary, et al. "Who Was St. John of the Cross?" *America Magazine*, 14 Dec. 2018, https://www.americamagazine.org/faith/2006/01/30/who-was-st-john-cross.

3. Cross, John of the, et al. *Dark Night of the Soul*. TAN Classics, 2010.

4."Andrew Peterson – the Silence of God." *Genius*, https://genius.com/Andrew-peterson-the-silence-of-god-lyrics.

5.Bradford, Tom. *Did the Messiah Speak Aramaic or Hebrew? (Part 2) by E.a.knapp*, https://www.torahclass.com/archived-articles/412-did-the-messiah-speak-aramaic-or-hebrew-part-2-by-eaknapp.

6."Home." *Lifeline*, https://suicidepreventionlifeline.org/.

ꓕ Chapter Six- Love And Dating: The Ultimate Quest For Boaz

Epigraph: "Love Isn't Complicated, People Are." *Mesmerizing Quotes*, 24 Apr. 2019, https://www.mesmerizingquotes.com/love-isnt-complicated-people-are/.

1. Clery, Laura, director. *Facebook Watch*, 31 Dec. 2021, https://www.facebook.com/laura.clery/videos/hilarious-halloween-workout/1767163450252739/. Accessed 1 Jan. 2022.

2.Israel, Ira. *How to Survive Your Childhood Now That You're an Adult: A Path to Authenticity and Awakening*, New World Library, Novato (California), 2017, p. 66.

3. Schultz, David Leo, director. *Raggamuffin*. 8 July 2014, https://www.amazon.com/Ragamuffin-Millennium-David-Leo-Schultz/dp/B01GWCJMDA.

4. Svoboda, Martin. "Aristotle Quote #1944553." *Quotepark.com*, https://quotepark.com/quotes/1944553-aristotle-it-is-of-the-nature-of-desire-not-to-be-satisfied/.

5. Rougemont, Denis de. *Love in the Western World*. Princeton University Press, 1983.

6. Zavada, Jack. "Explore 4 Different Types of Love in the Bible." *Learn Religions*, Learn Religions, 11 May 2020, https://www.learnreligions.com/types-of-love-in-the-bible-700177.

7. *Man Plans, and God Laughs | Psychology Today*. https://www.psychologytoday.com/us/blog/our-emotional-footprint/201602/man-plans-and-god-laughs.

8."The Meaning of Hesed: Hebrew for Love." *FIRM Israel*, 15 Oct. 2021, https://firmisrael.org/learn/the-meaning-of-hesed-hebrew-for-love/.

⊺ Chapter Seven- Perfectionism: The Silent Killer

Epigraph: "A Quote from East of Eden." *Goodreads,* Goodreads, https://www.goodreads.com/quotes/184186-and-now-that-you-don-t-have-to-be-perfect-you.

1. Manning, Brennan. *The Ragamuffin Gospel,* Multnomah Books, Colorado Springs, CO, 2015.

2. Schultz, David Leo, director. *Ragamuffin:* . 2014.

3. Schultz, David Leo, director. *God's Fool: A New Story About an Old Saint.* 2020.

4. "Neurotic Definition & Meaning." *Merriam-Webster,* Merriam-Webster, https://www.merriam-webster.com/dictionary/neurotic.

5. TEDxTalks, director. *YouTube,* YouTube, 24 June 2016, https://www.youtube.com/watch?v=pi4JOlMSWjo. Accessed 1 Jan. 2022.

6. "Calvin and Hobbes: Never in the History of Calming Down." *Tom McCallum,* 25 Aug. 2020, https://tommccallum.com/2017/10/19/never-in-the-history-of-calming-down-calvin-hobbes/.

7. "Contemporary Man Is Blind to the Fact That, with All His... at Quotetab." *QuoteTab,* https://www.quotetab.com/quote/by-carl-jung/contemporary-man-is-blind-to-the-fact-that-with-all-his-rationality-and-efficien.

8.Baker, Amy. *Picture Perfect: When Life Doesn't Line Up,* New Growth Press, Greensboro, NC, 2014, p. 11.

9. "Riddler." *Wikipedia,* Wikimedia Foundation, 20 Nov. 2021, https://en.wikipedia.org/wiki/Riddler.

10. Vischer, Phil, director. *Galaxy Buck: Mission To Sector 9.* 20 Oct. 2015.

⊓ Chapter Eight- Surrounded By Mirrors

Epigraph: "James Russell Lowell Quote: 'Whatever You May Be Sure of, Be Sure of This, That You Are Dreadfully like Other People.'". *Quotefancy*, https://quotefancy.com/quote/1302805/James-Russell-Lowell-Whatever-you-may-be-sure-of-be-sure-of-this-that-you-are-dreadfully.

1."The Snow Queen." *Wikipedia*, Wikimedia Foundation, 22 Dec. 2021, https://en.wikipedia.org/wiki/The_Snow_Queen.

2."R/Jung - Carl Jung Said 'Everything That Irritates Us about Others Can Lead Us to an Understanding of Ourselves.'". *Reddit*, https://www.reddit.com/r/Jung/comments/dxp8rp/carl_jung_said_everything_that_irritates_us_about/.

3.Langley, Liz. "Here's What Happens When a Chameleon Looks in a Mirror." *Animals*, National Geographic, 3 May 2021, https://www.nationalgeographic.com/animals/article/animals-chameleons-reptiles-science-colors.

4.Zimmer, Carl. "Children Learn by Monkey See, Monkey Do. Chimps Don't." *The New York Times*, The New York Times, 13 Dec. 2005, https://www.nytimes.com/2005/12/13/science/children-learn-by-monkey-see-monkey-do-chimps-dont.html.

5. "Three Blind Mice." *All Nursery Rhymes*, https://allnurseryrhymes.com/three-blind-mice/.

6.Buechner, Frederick. *Telling Secrets*, HarperSanFrancisco, San Francisco, 2004, pp. 26–27.

7.Eldredge, John. *Walking with God: Talk to Him, Hear from Him, Really*, Nelson, Nashville, 2008, p. 20.

8."Blog Archives." *THE ETYMOLOGY NERD*, https://www.etymologynerd.com/blog/archives/12-2017#:~:text=Sanctum%20has%20one%20of%20the,sehk%2C%20with%20the%20same%20definition.

9.Groth, Aimee. "You're the Average of the Five People You Spend the Most Time With." *Business Insider*, Business Insider, 24 July 2012, https://www.businessinsider.com/jim-rohn-youre-the-average-of-the-five-people-you-spend-the-most-time-with-2012-7.

ʊ Chapter Nine- Unwanted Gifts

1. Fritscher, Lisa. "Coping with the Fear of Long Words." *Verywell Mind*, Verywell Mind, 28 Feb. 2021, https://www.verywellmind.com/hippopotomonstrosesquipedaliophobia-2671752.
2."Understand the Facts: Anxiety and Depression Association of America, ADAA." *Anxiety Disorders and Depression Research & Treatment*, https://adaa.org/understanding-anxiety.
3."'The Longest Journey You Will Ever Take Is the 18 Inches from Your Head to Your Heart."." *Passiton.com*, https://www.passiton.com/inspirational-quotes/6679-the-longest-journey-you-will-ever-take-is-the.
4. "Billy Graham Quote: 'Anxiety Is the Natural Result When Our Hopes Are Centered in Anything Short of God and His Will."." *Quotefancy*, https://quotefancy.com/quote/775826/Billy-Graham-Anxiety-is-the-natural-result-when-our-hopes-are-centered-in-anything-short.
5.Becker, De Gavin. *The Gift of Fear: Survival Signals That Protect Us from Violence*. Dell Publishing, 1998.
6.Burkhalter, Stella. *Living Between Alpha and Omega: Praying the Greek Alphabet in Uncertain Times*, 2020, p. 55.
7. Yancey, Philip, and Philip Yancey. *Where Is God When It Hurts? ; What's so Amazing about Grace?*, Zondervan, Grand Rapids, MI, 2008, p. 37.

8. Lawrence, and Marshall Davis. *The Practice of the Presence of God in Modern English*. Marshall Davis, 2013.

˒ Chapter Ten-Pharisectomy

Epigraph: Haas, Peter Traben. *Pharisectomy: How to Joyfully Remove Your Inner Pharisee & Other Religiously Transmitted Diseases*, Influence Resources, Springfield, MO, 2012, p. 53.
1. "Nirvana – Smells like Teen Spirit." *Genius*, https://genius.com/Nirvana-smells-like-teen-spirit-lyrics.
2. Lewis, C. S. *Mere Christianity*, HarperOne, New York, NY, pp. 172–177.
3. Haas, Peter Traben. *Pharisectomy: How to Joyfully Remove Your Inner Pharisee & Other Religiously Transmitted Diseases*, Influence Resources, Springfield, MO, 2012, p. 139.
4. Ramis, Harold, et al. *Groundhog Day*.
5. Ckirgiss. "Sorry, but C. S. Lewis Never Said That There ." *Breathe*, 13 May 2015, https://crystalkirgiss.com/2015/05/13/sorry-but-c-s-lewis-never-said-that-there-in-which-i-begrudge-the-alarming-glut-of-authoritative-misquotes/.
6. Wiesel, Elie. *The Gates of the Forest*, Schocken Books, New York, 1996.
7. Spangler, Ann, and Lois Tverberg. *Sitting at the Feet of Rabbi Jesus: How the Jewishness of Jesus Can Transform Your Faith*, Zondervan, Grand Rapids, MI, 2018, p. 33.
8. "Woes of the Pharisees." *Wikipedia*, Wikimedia Foundation, 6 Oct. 2021, https://en.wikipedia.org/wiki/Woes_of_the_Pharisees.

˒א Chapter Eleven- There's A Hole In The Bucket

Epigraph:
https://www.azlyrics.com/lyrics/verticalhorizon/everythingyouwant.html

1. *There's a Hole in the Bucket: Traditional Children's Song Lyrics and Sound Clip,* https://www.songsforteaching.com/folk/theresaholeinthebucket.php.

2. "Read the Bible. Understand It. Apply It. Make It a Habit." *Through the Word app,* 22 Oct. 2020, https://throughtheword.org/.

3.Bernock, Danielle. "What Are the Names of God Found in the Bible?" *Christianity.com,* Christianity.com, 8 June 2020, https://www.christianity.com/wiki/god/what-are-all-the-names-of-god.html.

4.Church, Community Bible, director. *Facebook Watch,* 6 Dec. 2020, https://www.facebook.com/cbcsocial/videos/3479647015444803. Accessed 2 Jan. 2022.

יב Chapter Twelve- Chronicles

Epigraph: "Quotable Quotes: The Doctor Matt Smith." *Goodreads,* Goodreads, https://www.goodreads.com/quotes/902620-we-are-all-stories-in-the-end-just-make-it.

1."Books of Chronicles." *Wikipedia,* Wikimedia Foundation, 27 Dec. 2021, https://en.wikipedia.org/wiki/Books_of_Chronicles#:

2."The Sense of Ending: What Is Real Last Book of the Old Testament?: Bibleproject™." *BibleProject,* https://bibleproject.com/blog/sense-ending-real-last-book-old-testament/.

3. Waters, Roger, director. *Roger Waters: The Wall.* 6 Sept. 2014.

4.MB;, Liester. "Personality Changes Following Heart Transplantation: The Role of Cellular Memory." *Medical*

Hypotheses, U.S. National Library of Medicine, https://pubmed.ncbi.nlm.nih.gov/31739081/.

5.Strong, James, and James Strong. *The New Strong's Expanded Exhaustive Concordance of the Bible*. Thomas Nelson, 2010.

6. Wachowski, Lilly, et al. *The Matrix*. 24 Mar. 1999.

Acknowledgments

To my Sun and Moon, Brandon and Hunter:
"I love dew too"

Shyann and Shelby- You might not have come from my womb but you are always in my heart. Never forget how much Jesus loves you.

Dad, Mom, and Cary: I love you three so very much. Thank you for not killing me as a teenager. I promise I will try my best to not put you in a nursing home in return.

To Kurt, Julia, Leon and Mara: I love you four! I have the most adorable nephew and niece. I'm not biased or anything because they really are the cutest.

To all my extended family: There isn't enough space to tell you all how much I love and appreciate you all. YOU ARE LOVED!

Lisa: Thank you for loving my boys like your own. I appreciate you more than you know.

Shayne: Psalm 34:18. Praying for you always.

Johnna: Your voice matters more than you know. Iron sharpens iron. Shake and bake!

To all my girls: Avery, Danielle, Colene, Kim, Cara, Laura, Amy, JoAnna, Kristy, Rachel, Christi, Angel, Amanda, Cynthia, Charlotte, Anna, Kara, Jessica, Kristen, Jodi, Svannah, Modesta, Grace, Valerie, Kate, all my Emmaus Sisters, my Cowboy Fellowship small groups, Johnson Street ladies, my D1 family, and everyone else I might not have named. Iron sharpens iron, and I have some mighty sharp Sisters!

Thank you to Michael and Cindy McFarland, and their entire office "staph". You all have been such a light in a dark time. Never lose your enthusiasm for life.

Thanks to Jackie for being the best sponsor ever. You are such a gangster for Jesus and I hope to be like you one day. Love you!

To Felica: I look forward to folding fitted sheets in heaven with you. Love you Sister!

To Paul Jones for making IHOP truly the International House Of Prayer and for always making me smile you magical mystic beast.

Thank you Tonya for all the good conversations over coffee. We are kindred spirits who desire to share Christ's love to the world through our art. I can't wait to read your next book!

To all my Ragamuffin family who represent what it truly means to live in God's grace and for showing me how to breathe again. "Who told you that?"
Thanks TB for being my prayer warrior and the mirror to my soul. Stop beating yourself up.

Community Bible Church (CBC) and Cowboy Fellowship for being my family.

Toda Daniel and Anne Boley at Baruch HaShem for being my מורים the past couple years. The seeds you plant for the Kingdom produce more fruit than you know.

Thank you to Audrey and Kevin McCleary for letting me share how Tanner and Madi's story briefly intertwined with my story. Your strength inspires others more than you know.

Ry guy, I know you hate me now but I will always love you Brother.

Love you always K.K.

Havilah Cunnington and her ministry for her Crash Course to Communication class on how to write a book. I couldn't have made this dream come true without her! Enroll here at: https://theinfluencertable.com/writeabook/

Thank you Kat Bailey, for embarking on the journey to edit this beast. Couldn't have done it without you.

To Mrs. Verna Mae Byrd: I can't wait to see your glorified body in heaven. A lot more people are rejoicing in heaven because of you.

To LB: Thank you so much for being a bright light in a dark time. We're all doing our best.

ABOUT THE AUTHOR

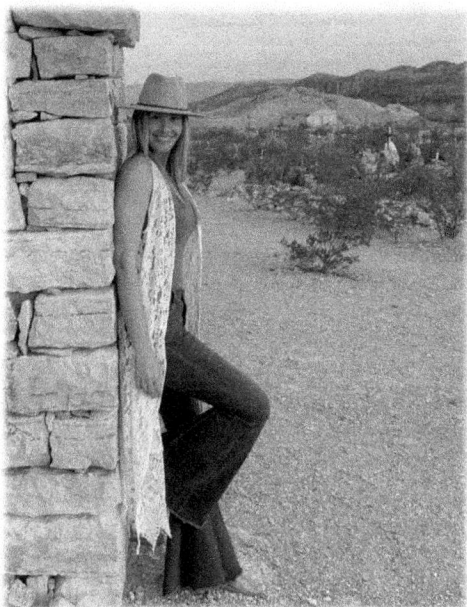

Single mother, book lover, author, blogger, recovering addict/perfectionist Tasha Page is a born-again Christian who is chasing after Jesus with all her heart, soul, mind and strength. She attends church at Community Bible Church (CBC) in San Antonio, TX. At the time this was published she is enrolled in her second year of Biblical Hebrew classes at Baruch HaShem. Her next goal is to learn Koine Greek.
We shall see!
To learn more about her online community for other Christian book lovers, go to www.TashaPage.com